POLITICS AND AMERICAN POLICING:
THE 'protect and to serve' Travesty

Kevin Michael Hermes

2010

Dedication

To all those who aspire to command law enforcement officers, remain true to your chosen profession by always demanding the utmost in integrity of yourself, your staff and the officers who serve with you. One of the greatest law enforcement executives of our time, former Police Chief Daryl F. Gates, of the Los Angeles Police Department, personally offered his advice to the author, "The troops need strong thoughtful leadership; they need to know when they are wrong and really need to know when they are right, take good care of them." Carry this credo with you throughout your law enforcement career and you cannot fail. Do not succumb to the politics of the day and remain cognizant that justice is blind and shall be upheld in the most equal and balanced manner.

ABSTRACT

The purpose of this book is to examine political influence within America's police and its founding impact upon policing formation and practices. The writing brings together a compilation of literature from peer-reviewed journal articles, incorporating a multidisciplinary approach, borrowing from the fields of sociology, history, political science, criminology and criminal justice. Through the use of secondary resources, this examination of historical fact and empirical study comes together that posits the hypothesis that America's police was founded within the realm of the political power elite. Those who controlled politics and the economy, from a historical perspective, sought nothing more than to protect and serve their own elitist interests through political influence and power, so as to keep the threat of social disorder in control amongst the lower classes. Such a coercive foundation has formulated the strategies and deployment of policing within the United States as we know it today. The writing does recognize the notable historical foundations of organized policing and ideologies that have been built upon as constructed by English precedent.

Table of Contents

Introduction...5

Chapter I Early Foundations of a Mechanism of Control for the Body Politic

- *Economic Growth and the Concept of Policing*.....................10

- *Henry Fielding and the Need for State Control*.....................16

- *Emile Durkheim, Anomie and the Threat Against the Organ of Government*..22

Chapter II Politically Organized Policing

- *The English Foundation*..27

- *The Birth of America's Police*..32

- *The Political Machines versus the Reformers at the Turn of the Twentieth Century*..36

Chapter III *The* Twentieth Century and the Entrenched Reality

- *Contemporary Police Design*...43

- *The Inequitable Delivery of the Quantity of Law*.................47

Chapter IV The Police and Crime Control: Pawns in a Political Game

- *Political Rhetoric and its Very Real Affect Upon Policing*........54

- *Presidential Influence*..62

- *Community Policing: A Political Fad*....................................66

- *Bratton's Success Story: When Competent Police Leadership and Expertise Come Together Autonomy can Prevail*............................70

Conclusion The Protect and to Serve Travesty.......................76

References...80

Introduction

To protect and to serve; the all too familiar motto that has indirectly become the ideological foundation of police all across the United States. Little did Officer Joseph S. Dorobeck, of the Los Angeles Police Department, realize at the time back in 1955, when he entered his short, five word clause into a departmental contest seeking a motto for the police academy, that it would capture the ideals of the police mission throughout the nation and build upon a perceived national institution into the twenty-first century (The origin, 1963).

Most would advocate that the police are a national institution. The author posits that it is the idea of the police, rather than the police themselves, that is a national institution, which was given birth by a growing political economy that saw urbanization, immigration, racial tension and the development of social stratification as spawning disorder, thus creating an ever-present threat of collapse.

As the growth of humankind expanded into varying cultures and organized societies, economies began to take shape as structured by governmental systems. These organized societal systems established norms and mores as to what was perceived as accepted living conditions among its people, along with what was to be considered morally right and morally wrong regarding social order and property rights. "Society in this case refers to the individual, collective, public, private and state and/or market combinations that shape the institutional arrangements for provision and help generally defined social order" (Daleiden, 2006, p.603). As early as 1651, English Philosopher Thomas Hobbes, revered by many political scientists still today, saw the need for the power establishment to control social contracts and property rights as expressed in his work entitled *Leviathan*. Hobbes suggested that sovereignty and social freedoms could not be pursued without a coercive arm of the government overseeing such (2006). As economies progressed, the concept of the police and policing became more evident among political philosophers as protectors of the growing economic condition that paralleled the body politic. Some of the notable early scholars of the eighteenth century included English jurist Sir William Blackstone and Scottish economist Adam Smith, who both advocated the need for a public police, although Smith was skeptical about policing in a centralized format (2006). During this time classical political economic philosophy pronounced that social order could be controlled through a free market system by a laissez-faire state, however, classical economists did not undermine the importance of a police creation to protect the state.

Such genius political philosophies created an avenue of emergent concern that organized policing eventually became a reality in early nineteenth century England when Sir Robert Peel was permitted by parliament to create the London Metropolitan Police in 1829 (Daleiden, 2006). With the advent of Marxian and neoclassical economic philosophies in the middle to latter half of the nineteenth century, the concept of organized police became ever so present across the ocean following its English roots.

The United States was initially slow to recognize the need for organized policing after the birth of the new nation. As urbanization grew, immigrants poured in and the melting pot was overflowing with economic growth coupled with social disorder. The City of Boston is credited with having the first organized police force in the nation in 1838 (Miller, 2000), although only charged with the responsibility of patrolling the streets during the day; sprawling New York City was soon to follow. Machine politics became the norm within these congested urban jungles that controlled largely immigrant local groups that supported a gambit of vice that involved gambling, prostitution, and an abundance of alcohol consumption. The police were bought and paid for and tolerated the drunken state of affairs as requested by the politicians in control.

Religious based morality had subsided and the police were accepting of what was perceived as the legitimate ills of urbanization. The influx of immigration and growing racial and cultural tensions within the United States at the turn of the twentieth century brought about the rise of a class of citizen that saw themselves as the true Americans, the top of the social strata, not newly arrived immigrants, and not part of the local political machines, rather as upper class reformers who saw a government that was losing control and in jeopardy of crumbling as the nation's capitalistic economy grew. Sociological writings from Emile Durkheim, whom many labeled the father of sociology, gave rise to the fact that society could be lost with what he termed as anomie, being described as a breakdown of societal norms and a loss of social restraint (Smith, 2008). The onset of the twentieth century was the beginning of the reform era where the upper-class, non-immigrant took back societal control and reformed the police mission. However, the changes in policing during this time were often brutal and lacking in any form of standardization among the varied agencies that were growing in number throughout the nation. Once again, a call for reform within policing was sought; this time it was professionalism that was on the horizon. Despite some scholars who advocate that the professional era of policing, as witnessed in the mid-twentieth century, removed the police from political influence, the author disagrees; the political leash tightened around the police and became an entrenched reality of policing in America.

The twentieth century brought numerous changes for America's police. A more organized structure, civil service reforms and further notable scholars were on the rise with notions of causations of society's deviant behaviors from famed sociologist Robert K. Merton and notable academician James Q. Wilson. Additionally, the body politic in the United States steadily grew stronger. Protecting the government was paramount and threats could not be tolerated to either the nation or the individual politician from the varying and solidifying differences among the social strata. The words of politicians became enflamed with rhetoric of social control, changes to the police, crime and punishment. The politicians' mere words, although often not amounting to anything substantive, developed into an expected political theme carrying into the twenty-first century. This powerful political rhetoric, throughout the twentieth century, too often gave way to symbolic changes in police policy and empty endeavors designed for nothing more than to win an election. The advent of community policing in the latter half of the twentieth century is one such example of nothing more than a political fad.

The contemporary police executive has became a political pawn that sees fit to succumb to the politics of the day and place his/her years of expertise on a dusty shelf, leaving the officers served as well as the community behind; it has become an expected and tolerated norm of the police executive within the United States. However, periodically there is a leader that comes along that reminds us how to find that balance between politics and policing and remain true to the profession; this can be seen in William Bratton's New York City success story.

Little did Los Angeles police officer Joseph S. Dorobeck realize back in 1955 that his beautifully crafted motto, that encompassed the ideals of the Los Angeles Police Academy, was already a well-founded guise by the body politic for the conceptual creation of the police nearly 126 years earlier when the first London Bobbies took to the streets.

Chapter I

Early Foundations for a Mechanism of Control for the Body Politic

Without an organized coercive arm of the power establishment like a government, chaos and anarchy would result in a war of all against all.

> *Thomas Hobbes, 1651*
> *Leviathan*

Economic Growth and the Concept of Policing

To gain a better understanding as to what led to the birth of a police concept an early examination of political ideologies, with respect to state control of a fragile yet growing economic condition is required. The growth of political economies spawned the concept for the need of "...an organized coercive power establishment... [To protect] ...social freedoms...enforce contracts and property rights" (Daleiden, 2006, p.604), as noted in Thomas Hobbes' scholarly writings entitled *Leviathan*, 1651. Additional scholars, such as English jurist and legal scholar Sir William Blackstone (1723-1780) and philosopher and economist Adam Smith (1723-1790), both contributed to the necessary notion for a policing concept. The growing complexities of varied political economies among growing states in the seventeenth and eighteenth centuries ignited the writings of political philosophers to pronounce the need for the concept of a policing body. Classical, Marxian and neoclassical political philosophies, as well as the early political thought of Aristotle, deserve to be examined due to their contributions to the body politic as we know it today and its institutionalized guardian – the police.

Before moving forward, a greater understanding of what a political economy constitutes is necessary. A political economy may refer to the methodology utilized by a particular state or society for the provision of various goods to its citizenry through political and economic means. Additionally, a political economy will provide for the dictates regarding what are socially accepted practices that govern the trade of commerce as well as property rights. In other words, the state will determine what is simply right and what is wrong. Therefore, presumably, a society can be defined as "the individual, collective, public, private, and state/or market combinations that shape the institutional arrangements for provision and help generally defined social order" (Daleiden, 2006, p.603).

Aristotle (384-322 BC) wrote extensively on the nature of political economic states in his book V, *Politics* and his book VI, *Histories*. Aristotle described three distinct types of governments where the rule of law could dictate: a state ruled by one, known as a monarchy, a state ruled by a few, known as an aristocracy, and a state ruled by many, known as a democracy. However, all three states were cautioned due to the ever-present threat of collapse if a state lost control in that the rule of law would become a state of irrational will by the people or the rule of law would become force by the state and the result would be tyranny, oligarchy or anarchy respectively (Dodsworth, 2006). According to Aristotle, the only preventative method for avoiding such a societal demise "…was to mix all three forms of government, which would hold one another in balance by opposing the tendency of each one to dominate the others" (2006, p.442). The Roman Empire was one such example of Aristotle's mixed form of government incorporating a monarchy, aristocracy and a democracy, however, its collapse proved as an historical lesson learned for future civilized political economic states. However, the Roman concept of the rule of law as a means of social control, as distributed through a coercive arm of government for the protection of social order, has sustained.

What had been established to date was the necessity for social order as provided by the political economic state. The body politic was perceived as the institution that was now the protector of the political economy and the enforcer of the law. It was this very ideology and sense of self-preservation as a necessary requirement that was pronounced within the philosophically heightened period known as the Enlightenment of the eighteenth and nineteenth centuries. The Enlightenment period brought about the political economic philosophies of the classical, Marxian and neoclassical political economic thought.

11

Classical political economy supported the idea of a laissez-faire state in which a free market economy would ultimately produce social order through the establishment of wealth for all members of society. "In autonomous fashion, markets would ideally grow in size, where supply would create demand based upon prices for goods that would be self-sustaining. Through a division of labor, resource distributions would be generated to allow for savings and investment in addition to consumption" (Daleiden, 2006, p.610). Classical political economic philosophy however, did not place aside the need for a protector of the economic condition. As noted in his writings entitled, *Commentaries on the Laws of England*, English scholar Sir William Blackstone, 1765, described specifically the police as, "the public police and economy" (2006, p.611), thus referring to an organized body of police to protect the community from not only murder and property crimes but equally as protector to the "...public infrastructure" (2006, p.611). The parallel between the economy and its requirement for protection as provided by the state was becoming more apparent in the politically charged philosophical writings of the 1700s.

Another notable philosopher during the period was Scottish economist Adam Smith (1723-1790). Often referred to as the father of laissez-faire economic theory, Smith provided two basic tenets regarding the ideologies behind the policing concept which are still held as true foundations today in his book, *Lectures on Justice, Police, Revenue and Arms*, in 1763. Smith advocated for a form of policing as protector of the economy, however he was skeptical of a centralized body of police, which coincides with Smith's first tenet that policing *quality* was far more paramount and effective than policing *quantity*. By comparing Paris, which at the time had a more centralized sense of policing with greater quantity of personnel, yet had higher crime rates, to London, which had a lesser degree of a centralized policing effort and yet had lower crime (Daleiden, 2006), Smith put forth the quality of effective policing versus the quantity of

12

police personnel argument which is still supported today in many jurisdictions throughout the United States, where the utilization of effective strategy, rather than population alone, determines the necessary allocation of the number of police personnel. Secondly, Smith advocated that a prosperous economy creates a division of labor, thus creating a "cheapness or plenty" (2006, p.611), referring to a distribution of goods, which would in turn decrease the need for one to commit crime. Today's economic and crime prevention theories mirror such a philosophy in that if people are working and contributing toward the economy and have essentially busy lives they will have less time nor desire to commit crimes. Interestingly, Smith put forth in his book, *Wealth of Nations,* 1776, that it was the duty of the sovereign state to provide for a system of justice that would be financed through taxation (2006). Smith's writings led to the foundation of government taxation to financially support a public police.

Marxian political economic philosophy naturally was derived from the writings of Karl Marx (1818-1883). Marxian ideologies indirectly had a great impact upon the recognized need for the state to create an organized police for the protection of the economy. In *Capital – Volume 1,* 1867, Marx "makes reference to police as being a method to increase the accumulation of capital by increasing the exploitation of those in the labor classes, [thus exemplifying] Marx' main objections about free markets, as being capable in achieving a stable and lasting method of social order" (Daleiden, 2006, p.609). Marx disagreed that a free market economy with less government regulation, as seen within a laissez-faire state, could provide for wealth distribution and social order effectively. He advocated a clear and precise distinction in social class between the working proletariat and the bourgeoisie, who would struggle over economic resources, possibly creating additional differing social classes that would eventually succumb to violence amongst each other. One such example of Marxian philosophy that became reality was the labor

13

riot that took place in Chicago's Haymarket Square in 1886, where striking workers battled with police, numerous police and civilians were killed and injured (Parrish, 1994). The incident sparked turmoil within the national labor movement for over one year across the United States 1994).

Marx, like economist Adam Smith, contributed two essential tenets toward the concept of policing that continue to prevail. First, Marx spoke of the police as an institution of the state that was to be specifically utilized to maintain the existence of differing socioeconomic classes. Secondly, Marx takes a very different approach by offering a police concept that involves professionalism, legality, reforms, and employs community relations (Daleiden, 2006). Marx' second approach reflects the notion of community policing as initiated in the twentieth century; however, Marx' first concept is more fitting as the police became more organized and centralized, with respect to the varied localities that spawned across the United States. The concept of community policing is very much alive throughout the nation as the twenty-first century progresses, to which many police agencies claim that they partake in the questionable strategy. The community policing concept will be discussed further in Chapter IV.

Neoclassical thought initiated in the latter-half of the nineteenth century. The main premise of the political economic theory was a focus upon "...the demand side of economic behavior and less on matters of earlier classical oriented supply" (Daleiden, 2006, p.613). Both classical and neoclassical theorists expressed the importance of the individual within the market economy. The classical theorists supported the individual as a vital component to the division of labor, whereas the neoclassical theorist supported the individual as a component within the economy, to which the individual would make decisions based upon influential factors. Examining the current economic condition, the individual would then determine one's own economic value and place

14

(2006). In other words, the individual makes economic choices based upon perceived cost and benefit analysis. But, inefficiencies will occur when one benefits from a market trade and another loses. This trend will expound when more persons get involved in such an economy to include the state, which in turn, will eventually lead to class conflict.

A notable theory that was brought forth by neoclassical thought, directly relating to a police concept, was an earlier notion as presented by economist Adam Smith, public goods theory. "Public goods theories help define the positive nature and dynamics of market and state institutional arrangements" (Daleiden, 2006, p.614). This political emphasis on public goods theory can be found within Smith's writings regarding the "duties of the sovereign" (2006, p.614), referring to an institution of justice being the state's overall financial responsibility through a collective funding. The neoclassical design compounded upon the earlier concept of Adam Smith that a police body not only was needed but should be funded through a public taxation. Therefore, the police, then, are perceived as a public good as provided by the state, which is considered a "non-excludable and non-divisible public police and safety good" (2006, p.615). The importance of these involved cohorts, being the political economic condition, the state and the police, is that a state controlled public good is distributed through political influence as to its level of quantity and quality upon the public.

The result of a state's economic growth and condition has directly influenced the concept of the need for an organized police to protect the state's interest, that being social order for self-preservation. Now having a greater understanding of classical, Marxian and neoclassical political economic thought as well as the definition of a society, a definitive statement regarding the police function is required. Can the police be defined as "those organized forms of order-maintenance, peacekeeping, rule or law enforcement, crime investigation and prevention and

15

other forms of investigation and information-brokering" (Zedner, 2005, p.82)? The definition offered is more so a description of the police activity, so often found in similar variations among so-called definitions of the police. A truly defined statement of what the police are must incorporate the fact that the police are a non-excludable, non-divisible public good and the interests that are protected and served must be duly noted. The author's definition of the police is as follows; the police are a non-excludable, non-divisible public good that are to protect and to serve social order in the interest of self-preservation for the existing body politic. This definition clearly exemplifies the cohort type relationship between the police and the state and the fact that "police reform then derives from the state's need either to combat growing political unrest or to discipline a new industrial labor force" (Harris, 1999, p.111).

Henry Fielding and the Need for State Control

English novelist and theorist Henry Fielding (1707-1754) is a vital component toward providing a historical foundation of support for the current hypothesis that America's police was founded within the realm of the political power elite, so as to keep the threat of social disorder in control amongst the lower classes. Fielding strongly advocated that social control was not only the responsibility of the state but that it was an imperative mandate. Fielding incorporated within his writings the ideologies of Greek philosopher Aristotle (384 BC– 322 BC), Marcus Cicero (106 BC- 43 BC) and John Locke (1632- 1704). Fielding's world was encroached with urban decay that filled London with various forms of vice; he believed that London was losing control to the lower classes. The ever-present urban decay that encompassed Fielding's world provided the impetus that is so prevalent throughout his writings, to instill within his government the realization that a lack of social control would ultimately lead to the state's demise.

16

During his tenure as a magistrate serving London in the mid-eighteenth century, Fielding was exposed to the social decay that urbanization was producing within the lower classes. In his writings to parliament on the issue of crime prevention within his work entitled *Enquiry into the Causes of the Late Increase of Robbers,* 1751 (Dodsworth, 2006), Fielding expressed that the need for police was significant due to his notion that distinct social classes and the alleviation of dependence upon the lower classes, as urbanization and technological advancements became more prevalent, increased the responsibility of the government to maintain social order. "The vast torrent of luxury which of late years hath poured itself into this nation" (2006, p.442), exclaimed Fielding. His unorthodox view of the causation of crime was not the result of a greater and concentrated populous nor the result of a greater division among social classes as a result of urbanization in eighteenth century London, rather crime causation was due to the "fact that the poor had been emancipated from their condition of dependence, [which] threatened order not in an abstract way, but in its practical effect on manners and government" (2006, p.442). In this sense, Fielding most likely would have supported the descriptive definition of police as noted earlier, the police are "organized forms of order-maintenance, peacekeeping, rule or law enforcement, crime investigation and prevention and other forms of investigation and information-brokering" (Zedner, 2005, p.82). Again, this definition of the police lacks an explanation as to why the police actually exist. But, Fielding made it clear what he thought the police role should be and its existence was necessary to keep the social classes distinct and in their proper places for the preservation of the body politic.

Clearly, Fielding was concerned that the neoclassical political argument regarding freedom and the state, if achieved, would be the demise of the state; "...liberty was defined not simply as freedom from interference, but as freedom from dependence or domination" (Dodsworth, 2006,

17

p.442). A self-governed freedom was not a practical possibility in a state that continued to witness urban growth coupled with an increase in vice, giving the lower classes, according to Fielding, an accumulation of wealth and dependence, which in turn gave rise to crime. Reflecting on Aristotle's writings in his book V *Politics* and his book VI *Histories,* Fielding saw Britain as succumbing to the historical demise as witnessed among other nations with respect to their rise and fall to power and freedom and back to luxury and slavery. According to Fielding, Britain, too, was traveling down this self-destructive road as depicted by Aristotle due to its exercise in growth and neglect. He exclaimed to parliament that such neglect has provided the lower strata a "…popular license, which could threaten the state from the democratic end of the spectrum…" (2006, p.442)

Strong government authority was required to maintain social order. Fielding put forth the political philosophy of Cicero, as stated in his writings, *In Catilinam* (63 BC), "For the lusts of these men are no longer moderate and their wantonness is inhuman and unbearable, they think of nothing but murder, arson, and rape" (Dodsworth, 2006, p.443). The utilization of Cicero, as conveyed to parliament by Fielding, strongly advocated that government intervention was of immediate need and it was not to be perceived as a coercive arm of government, but rather the duty of the government to protect the people and the duty of the government to protect itself. Fielding stated, "Our whole discourse is intended to promote the firm foundation of the state, the strengthening of powers, and the curing of the ills of the peoples" (2006, p.443). This paternal sense of government and this mandated responsibility to watch over the people has prevailed into the twenty-first century and it is indeed the police that are the government's watchmen.

One of Fielding's most notable contributions to appellate law and the constitutional concept was his notion that the constitution was not a fixed document, as originally thought by early

18

English politicians, but rather a constitution should be perceived as fluid in nature. A constitution flows with the changes of the people, expressed Fielding, and it was as "variable as the climate" (Dodsworth, 2006, p.444). Yes, the constitution formed the body politic that includes the permanency of the executive and legislative authorities, however, equally vital to the institution of the body politic was the "customs, manners and habits of the people, which all coalesced to form the political body" (2006, p.444). These customs, habits and manners amongst the people flow like a fluid; therefore, the constitution must flow with the changes of the people while at the same time adapting to the necessary needs of the government. Fielding again noted Aristotle in book V, *Politics*, by suggesting that a "Disproportionate increase is also cause which leads to constitutional changes" (2006, p.444), meaning that the disproportionate level of social disorder that London was experiencing at the time called for legislative action through the implementation of necessary constitutional changes.

Fielding again drew from the political ideologies of another great influential philosopher, John Locke. Reflecting upon Locke's work in *Two Treatises of Government* (1690), Fielding noted that Locke supported change in the government as seen fit in his expression *Salus Populi Suprema,* meaning "the good of the people is the supreme law" (Dodsworth, 2006, p.444). Fielding was utilizing rhetoric so as to persuade parliament that rhetoric was a necessary component of the government in order to unknowingly persuade the citizenry to succumb to the supreme law of the land, which was in fact for the good of the people. Lockean ideology advocated a greater government control, which could be put forth under the guise as necessary and ultimately acceptable by the people, in almost any circumstance. Locke stated, "Whatsoever cannot but he acknowledge to be of advantage to the society, and people in general, upon just and lasting measures, will always, when done, justifie itself [sic]" (2006, p.444). In other words, any action required by the government was necessary for the good of the people and the people could be made to believe in such action. It is here where it can be conceived through Fielding's use and compilation of early political philosophers, within his own political ideologies, that political rhetoric had been given birth in a contemporary sense. It is such rhetoric that influences the people regarding the need for governmental control of defined social strata for the betterment of the people and that any such action is indeed the will of the people. The United States Patriot Act of 2001 is a contemporary example of government action claimed to be under the guise of the will of the people in order to combat future acts of war (terrorism) upon the soil of the United States. The fluidity of the constitutional rights of the people were infringed upon, as perceived by many civil libertarians, by a government that capitalized upon the terroristic acts of war on September 11, 2001. Politicians all across the nation engulfed the public's perception with a plethora of political rhetoric that ignited extreme patriotism in order to support sought after executive and eventual legislative governmental action.

It is, therefore, the will of the people to control social order through the use of police. It is the politician who represents the people and must accept the responsibility to "…prevent the contagion from spreading to the useful part of mankind" (Dodsworth, 2006, p.445). Fielding suggested that the lower classes have been swallowed by the vice that urbanization had created; they are lost, yet they must be kept within their accepted place in society. It is the mind of the useful, productive member of the community that must not succumb to the same fate; this is the government's responsibility.

Charging a police organization with the responsibility of protecting the freedoms and liberties of the people, while at the same time preserving social order and protecting economic stability, is somewhat a contradiction; such an arm of the government will undoubtedly oppress and protect at the same time. Fielding was well aware of this juncture and accepted the price to pay for such control. Fielding proclaimed, "If I am to be assaulted and pillaged, and plundered; if I can neither sleep in my own house, nor walk the streets, nor travel in safety; is not my condition almost equally bad whether a licensed or unlicensed rogue, a dragoon or a robber, be the person who assaults and plunders me" (Dodsworth, 2006, p.446)? Fielding was clearly advocating that a police organization enforcing the law, although at times would undoubtedly stifle a true sense of freedom, was far better an oppression to accept within our lives than to be oppressed by the robber, the murderer and the rapist. Fielding continued by suggesting that the constant "threat of crime was itself a condition of unfreedom...to be free required the active intervention of the governor" (2006, p.447).

Fielding certainly exacerbated the definitive lines drawn between the social strata, which is offensive toward contemporary sensibilities. His arguments were degrading to the lower classes, however, such arguments continued to be utilized by Sir Robert Peel in his appeal to parliament for the need of an organized, paramilitary police structure which came to fruition in 1829 with the enactment of the Metropolitan Police Act. Peel argued, "Those opposing the new police on the grounds of liberty gave credit to some parts of the population for the possession for the enjoyment of much more liberty than they actually possessed" (Dodsworth, 2006, p.446). Peel, like Fielding, was suggesting that the people could acquire the oppression of governmental control so that they may live with peace of mind or be at the mercy of those who would seek to do harm. It is without doubt that Fielding's arguments, although crass at times, paved the way for a greater span of government control through the realization that the constitution can change as needed for the preservation of the political body and can be conveyed to the mindful people as a necessary component for sustained freedom. It is through these early "European visions of police, [that] the moral order was something which had to be actively created through the act of governing" (2006, p.452). To protect and to serve the will of the government had become a solid foundation for the necessity of a police structure.

Emile Durkheim, Anomie and the Threat against the Organ of Government

The French sociologist Emile Durkheim (1858-1917) is often referred to as the father of sociology, having been credited with establishing the study of sociology as a science among French academics. His contributions to the field of sociology at the end of the nineteenth century are invaluable. His writings support the current study with respect to his creation and understanding of the term that he coined as *anomie*, which parallels the need for government control due to the ill will of the citizenry.

Durkheim's major work in 1893, *The Division of Labor in Society* was a bold undertaking in that he attempted to conquer such subjects as political and cultural influences in varied occupations and "to describe the contours of modernity and to recommend a fix for societal disorganization" (Smith, 2008, p.336). Durkheim noted that in less civilized societies cultural groups were bound together by rules and traditions and there was little disorganization, little disagreement. However, it was the more structured, urbanized society, such as the nations that were in the heart of the Industrial Revolution during Durkheim's period, that were more apt to experience a breakdown of norms, mores and traditions. The evolution of modernity expounded a sense of individualism that demanded greater flexibility and sparked diversity in varied belief systems creating a downward spiral of morality (2008). Within this context, Durkheim invented the term anomie, meaning a total breakdown of societal norms and expected normative behaviors. Durkheim's realization was that people required social restraint, without such restraint

22

one could not entirely be free. In his 1897 work entitled *Suicide,* Durkheim wrote, "we need the moral regulation of society to control our naturally unlimited aspirations: without such restraint, we would be enslaved by our passions...unable to escape an endless pursuit, we would be condemned to a state of perpetual unhappiness" (DiCristina, 2000, p.486). With emphasis on social morphology, Durkheim "turned to the law as a concrete and objective indicator of morality...the law reflects the social organization and the cultural life of a society" (2008, p.336). It is clear that Durkheim was an advocate of social control and that such particular social control, similar to Fielding's sense of paternal responsibilities, rested with the government.

Interestingly, Durkheim saw that government needed to be especially vigilant in its own protection by creating law that might not necessarily offend nor affect the citizenry, but rather create law that would be designed to suppress direct threats to, as Durkheim phrased, "...the organ of government" (DiCristina, 2000, p.488). Durkheim suggested that because the government protects the common good of the people, acts that directly threaten the government indirectly threaten the continued existence of the common good. Therefore, "government authority...can achieve a somewhat autonomous existence in which it is capable of producing its own spontaneous actions" (2000, p.488). The government, according to Durkheim, was able to determine what actions by the people might indeed threaten the very existence of the government, outside of the people, thus creating its own laws for self-preservation. Equally as vital, these governmentally created laws may come with punishments that exceed the severity of the public conscience so as to ward off any temptation by the people to challenge the government.

Durkheim's existence of anomie within growing urbanized cultures and his ideologies regarding social control have greater importance upon the current hypothesis than what appears

23

upon the surface. Durkheim is an outsider, a strict academician not of a legal background or practitioner of the law; he is a self-proclaimed sociologist. Through his scholarly writings he promoted the importance of government control and the protection of its own interests. He was wary of a societal breakdown of norms and mores as cultures became more complex; his writings simply made sense. More importantly, he wrote at a time when organized policing was well under way throughout Europe and in the cities of the United States at the end of the nineteenth century. The political machines, as given birth by immigration and the Industrial Revolution within the United States, evidently incorporated Durkheim's ideals, although most likely indirectly. Durkheim's writings cannot be ignored when realizing that greater government control increased at the end of the nineteenth century along with the development of organizationally structured policing.

The need for social control was more apparent as populations grew and became concentrated as social class divisions became more distinct. Durkheim's redefined notion of anomie of the twentieth century, as carried forth by sociologist Robert K. Merton (1910-2003), had a significant impact upon the role of the police within the emerging criminal justice system in the United States. The complexity of society had indeed created a distinct class system, although the culture within the United States emphasized that success and wealth was available to all, the means for success did not fall equally across all social class lines. This frustration, this unavailability of opportunity experienced by minority groups ultimately results in anomie as defined by Merton (Merton, 1997). It is the police, as perceived by minority groups that are the strong arm of the government that indeed perpetuates oppression.

Durkheim's sociological writings of the nineteenth century and Merton's contemporary sociological writings of the twentieth century provided yet another wall to the foundation that

24

had been built upon by the earlier foundations of Blackstone, Smith and Fielding. It became evident that social control, through the development of law, was a required component of complex societies in order to protect the organ of government through structured, politically organized policing.

Chapter II

Politically Organized Policing

Decent people and bums are not equal.

James Q. Wilson, 1968
Professor of Government
Harvard University

The English Foundation

England's Metropolitan Police Act of 1829 is credited in most criminal justice circles as providing London with the first organized and centralized police force. Undoubtedly, Home Secretary Sir Robert Peel's efforts significantly contributed to the overall development of police organizational structure as it is known today. But the English effort does not solely commence with Sir Robert Peel's London Bobbies. English policing efforts in distinct, yet various forms can be found in the early eighteenth century. Local property owners largely depended on each other for the policing and prevention of thievery and other crimes against civilized peoples with the formation of volunteer policing efforts strictly for local protection. Such bands of watchmen and constables had neither cohesiveness nor conceptual standardization with respect to enforcement and punishment throughout the countryside. "The English saw inimical to freedom and preferred to punish the few than to police the whole of society" (Harris, 1999, p.111). They were repelled by the thought of a state organized policing structure similar to that of a standing army. However, the inevitable occurred, urbanization spawned, cities became far more complex and property owners could no longer respond adequately to the need for proper protection. The often politically perceived rogue bands of watchmen gave rise to the state to take control and accept its responsibility as the protectorate. The parallel between the earlier discussed political ideologies, coupled with the ongoing progress of policing the populous, comingled philosophy and the need to protect the government's self-interests, all came together to form an everlasting united institution by the state. The Bobbies were born out of the watchmen and the constables of years prior (1999). Many in England as well as the world saw the "...development of modern policing integrated with the development of new methods of class oppression: police reform then derives from the state's need either to combat growing political unrest or to discipline a new industrial labor force" (1999, p.111).

Eighteenth century policing in England was dependent upon property owners to protect their own interests, thus in turn protecting the interests of the state. "Institutions like the ancient hue and cry, still in existence in the mid-eighteenth century, required the men of a Hundred to go in pursuit of a felon once a constable raised the alarm" (Zedner, 2005, p.88). The position of constable was voluntary and all community members were expected to rotate the position with a commitment for one year. The Posse Comitatus, another form of policing as performed by the county sheriff, had the authority "to summon every person above 15 years old and under the degree of a peer to attend under pain of fine and imprisonment if they did not render their services" (2005, p.88). This unorganized method of controlling undesirable behavior within the state proved ineffective as urban areas began to sprawl and the populous grew. Additionally, the unpaid volunteers of the constabulary became less willing to participate due to an increase in population and an overwhelming increase in criminal behavior. Constables were willing to sell their services for continued protection among private interests. These services became profitable for the constable to which some magistrates sanctioned such solicitation of protection services and equally shared in the profits. Private industry began hiring constables for protection against their own employees whereas magistrates permitted the whipping of thieving employees outside the auspice of local justice. Policing was changing in the sense that it was viewed as a profit making business and corruption within the constabulary and the office of magistrate were together exchanging monies for personal interest rather than state interest. "...Protecting the profits of the manufactures took priority over ensuring that justice was seen to be done" (2005, p.88). Unfortunately, corruption in the public realm sustained and has become overwhelming in the American system of justice as witnessed today.

In the latter half of the eighteenth century growing concerns over protection became more paramount in England. The nation was not attending to its own self-interests through the regulation of social order and the ever-present threat of collapse in that the rule of law would become a state of irrational will by the people, as predicated by Aristotle, would eventually result. Private associations formed, outside of the constable for sale, where neighbors were protecting one another. For example, "the inhabitants of the Billingsgate Ward in London joined together to form a voluntary defense association for the protection of their neighbors and their property, by the exertion of every effectual legal method in the assistance of civil power, for the preservation of the public peace of this city" (Zedner, 2005, p.88). As these associations grew in number around London and throughout England, they became more organized and structured, although there was neither cohesiveness nor standard of application between neighborhood associations. Individually, the reputation of the members was accompanied with such characteristics as "propertied, articulate, able to mobilize themselves, and ready to defend their interests" (2005, p.88). The associations not only desired a public peace but equally so they desired overwhelmingly to keep out an ominous state control. However, it was the poor who suffered. Only the wealthy, the property owner and the rich put forth concern for their equals, the lower classes and the homeless were not perceived as a vital component toward society. The neighborhoods of the wealthy were safe, the lower classes were not and it was the state that realized the necessary responsibility to protect their own interests through a means of social control to avoid empowering the lower classes. The actions of the private associations actually gave birth to greater state control and failed in their attempt to maintain an avoidance of such control; "successful private efforts [had] expanded, not contracted public social control" (2005, p.88). The associations were innovated in their application toward protection, which in turn gave rise to "...new forms of social control [and] responsibility for which is, typically, then assumed by the state" (2005, p.88).

England moved forward fueled by the impetus found within the political ideologies of the Enlightenment. "Defending policing as a public good accords strongly with the eighteenth century neoclassical belief in policing as an integral aspect of civic virtue and a necessary precondition of liberty" (Zedner, 2005, p.88). Organized policing was becoming a necessity and it was on the horizon of the nineteenth century.

Many criminal justice scholars argue that organized and centralized policing did not exist prior to London's Metropolitan Police Act. The policing reforms that took place, as advocated by Home Secretary Sir Robert Peel during that period, were generally accepted by the public with somewhat ease and deemed not unconstitutional as many had for so long exclaimed, largely due to the fact that the watchman, the constable and the neighborhood association had been prevalent during the eighteenth century. "The Bobbies were not a new phenomenon, but rather eighteenth century watchmen and constables in new coats" (Harris, 1999, p.111). The Peelian reforms, however, regarding the need for a centralized form of policing, were not acceptable to every citizen. Peel brought his argument to parliament exclaiming that "...those opposing the new police on the grounds of liberty gave credit to some parts of the population for the possession for the enjoyment of much more liberty than they actually possessed" (Dodsworth, 2006, p.446). Peel, like Fielding, was suggesting that the people could acquire the oppression of governmental control so that they may live with peace of mind or be at the mercy of those who would seek to do harm, thus providing the criminal with greater freedoms.

Peel's Metropolitan Police Act came to fruition in 1829. Undoubtedly, Peel's efforts along with the first commissioner of the London Metropolitan Police, Sir Charles Rowan (Constantine, 2008) are to be credited with establishing a well-structured, organized and centralized paramilitary style police force that clearly has established the long lasting foundations found in American policing today. Their concepts were innovative and precise and their forethoughts are to never be categorized as anything but extraordinary. The Bobbies took to the streets of London as an unarmed, yet uniformed police force on September 29, 1829 (2008) providing social order for an expanding urban society within a clearly defined class system charged with the mission of protecting the social policies of London.

The Metropolitan Police Act can been perceived as the inception of the power elite taking control over social policy and prescribing the law as seen fit to suit the interests of the wealthy. The Metropolitan Police Act is the embodiment of the political ideologies of Aristotle, Blackstone, Locke, Smith and Fielding, thus revealing the fragility of a state and its very real sense of uneasiness with the intrinsic and definitive class system as created by their own economic culture. The possibilities were endless now. How far could this "locally-initiated social policy be applied beyond London [and should we] expect similar dynamics of change elsewhere" (Harris, 1999, p.112)? Thus, the new form of social policy recognized as organized policing did indeed find its way across the ocean to a young nation that was experiencing exploding industrialization and urbanization. The protect and to serve travesty became embedded as part of the democratic system within the United States and would be exacerbated to a level beyond anything that Sir Robert Peel could have ever possibly imagined.

The Birth of America's Police

The Puritans brought with them to the new world the religious based sense of social order that they were accustomed. "The holy enterprise of minding other people's business" (Miller, 2000, p.30) was the credo that the early settlers relied upon to live in peace. Community consensus was the foundation for social order where punishment through community shame, rather than policing, was the objective of warding off criminal or unwanted behavior. Upon England's defeat in the Revolutionary War, the people at all levels within the new nation absolutely forbid any concept that resembled a standing army for protection of the state and maintenance of social order. Order maintenance was left to local and county control with no centralized body governing policing efforts. Local and county policing efforts continued to parallel the growth of the nation as did political entities. Although policing eventually emulated a paramilitary structure, control over the police remained with the respective local political body. "Resultantly, the preference would ultimately create the unique foundation for the largest decentralized police system in the world" (Daleiden, 2006, p.612).

Policing colonial America mirrored English efforts, whereas the colonists incorporated much of the earlier concepts of the constable, the watchman and the sheriff; community consensus was still generally the law of the locality. These positions were considered voluntary, as were their English counterparts. However, American social conditions and political ideologies, of which much was taken from the political philosophies of the Enlightenment, evolved into American policing. Interestingly, the county sheriff was an appointed position and responsibilities were more so to collect taxes and supervise elections. The politicizing of the office of sheriff across the nation has remained the same today. Counties across the United States elect their county sheriff rather than being appointed by a local politician, but the candidate for sheriff must run a politically charged campaign as any other politician. Ironically though, this system has relieved the county sheriff, to some degree, of political control. The sheriff is elected by the people and does not have to answer to anyone but the people. A sheriff's only political repercussion is that of reelection.

With the influx of immigration the melting pot was taking hold and overflowing. The colonies expanded and port cities were slowly rising toward becoming entrenched politically controlled entities. The social climate had changed as well as the American culture as the nineteenth century got underway. People were becoming more private and demanded to be left alone within their homes and their lives; community consensus was no longer a viable option for protection. However, Americans in the north were skeptical to bring the English style police force to America. Their "democratic ideology prompted them to fear an institution imported from monarchial Europe" (Miller, 2000, p.31). It was this very fear that led to a desire by the American people to see that constables were to be appointed by local magistrates, local politicians or elected by the people. By demanding that early policing efforts be controlled through local politicians so as to avoid any similar concept of centralized state control, as compared to their English roots, Americans gave birth to a foundation of in-depth politically controlled, decentralized police forces all across the nation as well as at the soon to come federal level. Unknowingly, it would be this fear of monarchial control among the early settlers that resulted in the nemesis that plagues American law enforcement today, politics.

The south saw a very different type of policing effort much earlier than the northern cities, which claim to have the first organized police forces, such as Boston and New York City. Policing efforts in the south centered on the power elite and maintaining the noose of oppression around the neck of slavery. In the early nineteenth century "southern cities, such as Charleston and New Orleans...developed uniformed, heavily armed military style forces that swept the streets at night seeking disorderly or criminal slaves and free blacks" (Miller, 2000, p.30). The early development of such forces was created by the white power elite to maintain order and oppression among the growing slave population so as to avoid any inclination of an uprising.

The Jacksonian political era of the early 1830s, where all white men, other than property owners, demanded the right to vote, gave rise to the political elite in New Orleans to put forth increased yet innovative policing efforts. "New Orleans led the way in the national adoption of a plain-clothes, civilian day and night patrol force" (Miller, 2000, p.31). This force lacked any type of organized or centralized structure and only operated in areas of the city that were deemed as the greatest threat against those who sought to maintain political control (2000).

As the mid-eighteenth century was nearing, continued population growth and urbanization "played a significant role in justifying the need for public police systems" (Daleiden, 2006, p.612) all across localities throughout the nation. In 1838 the City of Boston is credited with having the first organized police force, although the force only initially patrolled the city during the day (Miller, 2000). It was New York City that was caught in political debates over the idea of organized policing until 1845. Largely modeled after the London Metropolitan Police, the civilian police force of New York City had its distinct American political influences in that local politicians appointed its members for limited terms (2000).

The Boston and New York systems grew and became an accepted and expected practice policing social order within the state and offering protection of the worthy citizenry. The immigrant explosion was well underway and could not be stopped. "Respectable citizens feared the mass immigration of the 1830s and 40s..." (Miller, 2000, p.31). Prisons were now a permanent fixture of the American justice system and the need for organized police forces became more apparent due to their ability to remove the "dangerous classes" (2000, p.31) from society and put them behind bars. The early fears of a monarchal like organized policing structure had dissipated to such a point that the middle and upper classes were calling for locally organized politically controlled police forces everywhere. "By the late nineteenth century, state (government) supported and operated policing became the social or public institutional norm" (Daleiden, 2006, p.612).

But, it was these calls for social control by local politicians that resulted in extreme levels of patronage and it was not long before the citizenry was again crying for reform in the latter half of the eighteenth century. New York's attempt at reform was the first to control the results of political control over the police through the establishment of civil service reform in 1857 through the implementation of civil service examinations for entry level police officers rather than the historical political appointment. Many jurisdictions throughout the nation still today employ a civil service system. But, it was evident that "the problem of political interference would not go away as long as the urban machines directly or indirectly controlled municipal institutions and profited from selective police enforcement in vice districts" (2000, p.32) throughout the various cities. The Americans of the eighteenth century called for it, politically controlled policing was now an everlasting and engrained component of American society.

The Political Machines versus the Reformers at the Turn of the Twentieth Century

As the twentieth century became a reality so too did the political machines that controlled the sprawling urban areas throughout the United States. Immigration was overwhelming to the hegemony middle and upper classes. "By 1900, the foreign-born population made up, on average, nearly one-fourth of the total population in the 50 largest cities and ranged as high as 48 percent" (Brown & Warner, 1997, p.294). The immigrant formed the labor class that was attracted to the Industrial Revolution. They brought with them their drunkenness, gambling and prostitution that many perceived as threatening the economic and political stability as controlled by the native-born respectable citizen and power elite. Their local and city-wide political machines dominated the political environment and as sought in earlier years, these very politicians controlled the police as well as their policing strategies or lack of. The progressive movement was in full-force supported by, whom they perceived themselves, as the respectable native-born citizen, who sought reform in all aspects of American culture to include the politically infiltrated police. This effort, however, was again nothing more than political infiltration upon the police that would develop into deeper and engrained political influences to include the nation's first "...political police agency to control radicalism and wartime spying" (Miller, 2000, p.33), the Federal Bureau of Investigation.

Although the twentieth century saw the breakdown of the community consensus of years past in controlling social order, there was still a sense of community among those who identified themselves as the respectable citizen of the time. They could be defined as "an amorphous group that ranged from bankers to brick layers" (Miller, 2000, p.33). This loose knit but ever-present middle and upper class native-born citizen perceived the growing immigrant population as a threat to their political strong holds and economic stability throughout the nation. "Their enemies

36

were the dangerous classes, equally amorphous…including…the Irish in the northeast during the 1850s or the Mexicans in the southwest during the 1940s [and] unskilled or casual laborers" (2000, p.33). Additionally, African-Americans were considered within this group of dangerous classes, but were at the lowest ranks of society and were always "…considered potentially, if not actually dangerous" (2000, p.33). Economic conditions of the 1890s created extremely tense relations between immigrant and native-born citizens. Intense labor conflicts resulted in many businesses failing or seeking out the cheaper labor offered by the immigrant in order to sustain capital in a failing economy. Labor demonstrations were seen on the landscape of nearly every major city crying for increased wages and better working conditions, yet the never-ending supply of newly arrived immigrants was quick to replace striking workers and to work under any conditions regardless of how horrific they were (Brown & Warner, 1997). It was the immigrant that contributed to urban decay, as perceived by the native-born citizen. Their vice-filled lifestyles were consumed with gambling, the gathering at saloons, prostitution and their excessive consumption of alcoholic beverages littered the city streets with drunks. "No social problem was seen at the root of more urban ills, no social problem was more associated with immigrant social life, and no social problem was more threatening to the middle and upper classes than intemperance" (1997, p.294). Additionally, for many immigrants they remained true to their customs and cultures, although many assimilated to American society, larger groups held on to their mores, norms and religious beliefs as they settled into American cities. It was these cultural differences that were often misconstrued as crimes "…because the legal culture of the state reflect[ed] the views of the dominant group" (Hasisi, 2008, p.1124).

Despite the negative characterizations made against the immigrant populous, they developed steadfast political machines both on the local, neighborhood level, commonly referred to as a ward, as well as within some city-wide political arenas. After the Civil War the nation was victim to rapid social and economic changes. The influx of the immigrant minority gave birth to an opportunity for those who sought to seek power through the use of patronage, favoritism, vice and corruption. "The city boss was a political capitalist entrepreneur whose main product was the provision of votes, a product manufactured with the reliability of a machine. In return, the political boss distributed the fruits of power to the organization's workers and the people in the neighborhoods they served" (Brown & Warner, 1997, p.295). The immigrants' social and economic concerns were taken care of through the use of the local political machine. It was the development of the political machine that infiltrated the police. Following established precedent, police officers were appointed by local politicians, who in turn would partake in the financial rewards offered by a variety of vice as governed by machine politics or ignore the growing social problems of urban decay that consumed the immigrant population. The police were indeed controlled by political machines throughout the United States; they were corrupt and ineffective in their protection efforts. "In the view of the native-born community...political bosses...embodied the political, economic, and cultural threats of the foreign elements of the city" (1997, p.295).

Such infiltration and corruption is evident in an examination of cities throughout the United States in 1900 comparing arrest rates for drunkenness. There were 70 fewer arrests per 10,000 people in cities that were considered to have a dominant political machine as compared to cities that did not (Brown & Warner, 1997). It was apparent that machine politics "...repaid immigrants and the producers and sellers of alcohol for their support by setting lenient police policies regarding alcohol and public intoxication" (1997, p.300).

However initially amorphous as the middle and upper classes were defined at the time, it was short lived for they created a movement of reform that swept the United States both culturally and politically, transforming a threatened political and economic system into a stronger, yet politically controlled system with a powerful hand; the Progressive era of the early twentieth century was well underway. Progressive reformers became a battlefront to contend with for the viable immigrant political machine, which eventually succumbed to the movement. But, in reality progressive reformers were nothing more than another political movement to control social order as they saw fit through the utilization of the police.

Infiltrating politics at the local, state and federal levels, progressive reformers sought and achieved change. For example, as early as 1857, New York was the first to implement civil service reform so as to combat the machine politics of patronage. Examinations became the requirement of those who sought police positions as well as promotions. Civil service reform led to a better quality applicant with higher intelligence and greater levels of integrity. As reforms took hold, the aggressiveness of the police was noted throughout cities that were once machine controlled, arrest rates rose for crimes that were once ignored such as drunkenness (Brown & Warner, 1997). Additionally, reformers achieved the passing of new laws as the twentieth century commenced that controlled alcohol consumption, closed saloons on Sundays and eventually got the 19th Amendment passed prohibiting the manufacture, sale or transportation of alcoholic beverages within the United States (Miller, 2000). These vast changes in social reform and police control employed one overall objective, to eliminate the immigrant threat.

One of the most controversial progressive reforms was that of the creation of what is known today as the Federal Bureau of Investigation (F.B.I.) in 1908. Literally, an investigative arm of the federal government, this politically designed police agency was the originator of Progressive

Era reformer President Theodore Roosevelt and his Attorney General Charles Bonaparte (History of the FBI, 2009). The well-known, and in some circles infamous, eventual director of the F.B.I., J. Edgar Hoover, created a law enforcement agency that influenced municipal policing nationally by developing a variety of standards for police operation. The federal arm of the law was well founded as the F.B.I developed into an investigative agency that became part of popular culture in 1930s, fighting against the all-too infamous gangster, fighting against the communist threat of the 1950s, investigating what was eventually coined as white-collar crime by sociologist Edwin Sutherland in the latter half of the twentieth century and today focusing on terrorism. The mission of the F.B.I. is indeed that of national security and will encompass any task that is necessary to protect the preservation of the United States government.

The Progressive Era reformers succeeded in taking political control of the police, creating what was called *professionalism* among the ranks. However, such professionalism resulted in strictly structured paramilitary police forces very much like Sir Robert Peel's London Metropolitan Police, which earlier Americans denounced and feared. "Crime fighting became the general order" (Miller, 2000, p.32), rather than social order maintenance. The goal was to limit political influence within the ranks of the police, but the result was quite the opposite when federal influence commenced in 1929. With President Hoover's appointment of the Wickersham Commission, which was given the task of investigating the causes of criminal activity and alcohol related influences across the United States, one such result of this report was the recommendation of extensive reforms within policing with respect to training, selection and education in addition to the recognition of the existence of widespread brutality as a deployed and accepted tactic among the policing field (2000). Federal influence had indeed been established within America's police, despite the growing number of agencies nationally on the municipal level. Decentralization was nothing more than a guise now that federal political influence had taken hold. The police had become more distant from the people served as the twentieth century progressed; their agenda was more clear than ever before in history; the police represented the white, majority, power elite and this evident characterization compounded in the middle twentieth century as witnessed with increased racial tensions and riots in numerous cities within the United States. Standard police procedure and design became the call of the majority and this indeed "…created unpredictable reactions in the minority community…" (Hasisi, 2008, p.1124).

Chapter III

The Twentieth Century and the Entrenched Reality

They should be held accountable, of course, but the manipulation of chiefs and police departments by political leadership has become excessive and has long been the stuff that corruption is made of; the process of silencing chiefs in today's America is almost complete.

> *Daryl F. Gates, 1992*
> *Los Angeles Police Chief*
> *1978-1992*

Contemporary Police Design

In 2006, University of California, Berkley, law professor David Alan Sklansky stated in an article entitled, *Private Police and Democracy*, "The police professionalism movement of the 1950s and 1960s succeeded so fully at insulating police departments from political interference that, even today... law enforcement often seems to operate outside the normal processes of local government, accountable to no one" (2006, p.90). This assessment of law enforcement and politics in the middle twentieth century, and as it progressed into the twenty-first century, certainly does not parallel with that of the reality as experienced by Los Angeles Police Chief Daryl Gates, as noted above, at the end of the twentieth century, nor does it parallel with what the political arena has established as contemporary police design.

Since their inception police organizations naturally and common sensibly interact with their environments. Interaction with the surrounding environmental factors such as the citizenry, political bodies, the criminal and the victim, albeit voluntary, forced or delegated, is an absolute within the world of policing. In the 1960s, this understanding of organizational interaction with the environment that encompasses them, thus ultimately shaping an organization's structure, came to be known as an open systems approach (Goltz, et al, 2008). An open system organization can be defined as organizations that "are necessarily and inescapably tied to the economy, political tides, perceived/real crises, demands from local citizens, and other related factors" (2008, p.178). How fitting this definition is in describing the twentieth century organizational structure of police agencies. An examination of the open systems definition will reveal the inescapable truths that encompass contemporary police design and the entrenched reality of political control.

43

The definition pronounces that organizations are "necessarily and inescapably tied to the economy [and] political tides...." This aspect of the definition clearly parallels the need for policing in that such a concept was established by Aristotle and economist Adam Smith, as mentioned earlier, whereas both philosophers spoke of the body politic as the institution that was now the protector of the political economy and the enforcer of the law. Interestingly, the definition's components noting that organizations are equally affected by "...perceived/real crises [and] demands from local citizens..." has indeed been the politics of the day that continuously places police agencies in a perpetual state of change that corresponds to their environments. It is the politics of the day that often exclaims crises for mere political gain that at times, in effect, really does not exist, but stimulates the people to ignition to such a point that they decry overwhelming concern and demand change. The power of political rhetoric to effect change within policing will be discussed further in Chapter IV. This is the open system design of a police agency of the twentieth century, which truly has been the essential ideology of policing since its inception; this is the politics of policing. After all, it was the body politic that created the police.

"Policing systems are not and cannot be closed off from their operating environment, but rather function much more efficiently and effectively when they are open to and dependent upon fluxuating resources, requests, and information from a diverse group of individuals and issues both inside and outside of the organization" (Goltz, et al, 2008, p.178). The author may argue with the notion that police departments function more effectively and efficiently at face value when they are open to and dependent upon fluxuating resources, requests, and information from diverse groups. Such "diverse groups" largely are politically motivated and have the necessary power to effect change so as to protect their own interests. Three distinct theories are evident

44

behind the impetus of political motivation that can directly affect policing: public choice theory, conflict theory and organizational theory (2008).

Public choice theory "assumes that governmental policies are influenced by public demand" (Goltz, et al, 2008, p.179). It is in fact the people who rise up and demand increased police personnel patrol the streets when crime rates soar. This demand will in turn empower the politician to allocate the necessary monies to increase the size of the respective police agency. It is suggested that public choice theory then "...is the result of public demand for social order, and evidence of police force growth corresponding to increases in the crime rate may be evidence of this perspective" (2008, p.179).

Conflict theory, to include economic conflict theory and racial conflict theory, is essentially economic inequality and unemployment as measures of class conflict (Goltz, et al, 2008). "As economically powerful groups have political power and thereby influence legislation and laws, the upper-class has more influence over the police than do other classes" (2008, p.179). This definition clearly offers support to the hypothesis that the police are nothing more than a coercive arm of the government to protect those in control and to keep in place "...marginalized populations" (2008, p.179).

Organizational theory suggests that the police organization is centered on politics and unionization and it is in fact its own organizational pressures that determine change or no change. In essence it creates its own "...organizational inertia" (Goltz, et al, 2008, p.179) that will determine effectiveness and strength of the organization.

In fact, the author posits that all three theories are centered on one vital component, politics. Politics, as mentioned earlier, is the science that created and sustains the state and it is the state that created the police. Public conflict theory is nothing more than the politician igniting the

45

public with respect to a perceived or real crisis, conflict theory is clearly the political power elite keeping the threat of the lower classes in their places so as to maintain state interests and organizational theory is the police themselves blinded by their own ignorance as to what their mission really is.

An additional examination of middle twentieth century police ideology supports the hypothesis that it is indeed the politics of the state that dictates police practices and design. James Q. Wilson's, 1968, *Varieties in Police Behavior* outlined three distinct styles of policing as set forth by the organizational design of the agency: the service style of policing, the watchman style of policing and the legalistic style of policing. The three distinct styles are evident in their respective titles. The service style is one of community-level service, where arrest is often the last resort, the watchman style emphasizes social order and crime prevention and the legalistic style is one of strict enforcement to maintain crime deterrence. All three styles, however, are predicated upon the political environment that the police service. It is the dictate of the political power elite coupled with the problems faced by the community as well as the concerns of the upper classes that will determine its law enforcement agency's policing style. Wilson noted that the "police are in all cases keenly sensitive to their political environment without in all cases being governed by it...[however]...the police may act independently in setting most policies and procedures but their agenda is set by municipal politicians" (Morabito, 2008, p.480). This is the protect and to serve travesty.

The Inequitable Delivery of the Quantity of Law

The protect and to serve travesty has been well established. This embodiment of the state is responsible for the delivery of social order and to control social unrest. The police, as defined earlier, are a non-excludable, non-divisible public good that are to protect and to serve social order in the interests of self-preservation for the existing body politic. In parallel to the current hypothesis that the police are state-controlled and serve the interests of the political power elite, it can be concluded that the police will deliver their services in an inequitable manner among the varied social strata. Donald Black, in his 1976 work entitled *The Behavior of Law,* concluded numerous theorizations regarding the manner in which the police respond and resolve calls for service based upon social strata to include: race, gender, wealth and education. Black's theories have been indirectly supported by empirical studies that ultimately support the current hypothesis, in addition to the fact that the police are not only state-controlled by the political power elite, but also deliver an inequitable quantity of law to the lower classes.

According to Black, "law is a quantitative variable whose quantity increases or decreases depending on powerful independent forces such as social stratification, morphology, culture… and non-legal social control" (Avakame, et al, 1999, p.766). In other words, Black's theories regarding the delivery of the law are dependent upon the independent variables, described above, that "…will influence the quantity of governmental social control" (1999, p.767).

The first independent variable is that of stratification. Black proposed, "the direction of the quantity of law is that law varies directly with stratification" (Avakame, et al, 1999, p.768). Social stratification is determined by one's culture. Stratification will be determined by one's wealth, educational level, age, gender and race, to name a few. The reality of social culture within the United States is that social stratification is ranked amongst its people from low to high. One is afforded more respect, generally speaking, in nearly every aspect of life when one is recognized as being of a higher social strata. Black's theory then implies that "people of higher rank have more law than those of lower rank; that is they are afforded better protection of the law, have greater access to law, and presumably are more willing to mobilize it" (1999, p.768).

Black's second independent variable is morphology, meaning the relational distance between people. Black, at the time, believed that the law was nearly nonexistent between intimate people, such as family members, believing that disputes were handled privately and the mobilization of the law was rarely, if ever, enacted. This perspective of legal intervention into the household amongst family members has indeed changed over the past three decades, largely with respect to the recognition and need for the development of domestic violence laws throughout the nation. However, during the time of Black's writings he was correct in theorizing that mobilization of the law was "…virtually inactive among intimates" (Avakame, 1999, p.769). Black continued to proclaim that the greater the relational distance between people, utilization of the law as a resort of resolution was increased. However, it must be noted that Black contended that differentiation within societal structure played a role as well. The higher strata individual who witnesses a crime against a lower class person might not be as compelled to notify the police, whereas if the same upper class individual witnesses a crime against another of the same upper class strata, then notification of the police will be more inclined (1999).

The third independent variable is that of culture. Culture sets one's identity, ideologies, and customs and often determines one's educational level. According to Black, "people with more culture - the well-educated, for example – are more contentious than others and are more keenly aware of their rights, social positions, and options" (Avakame, 1999, p.770). It is the well-cultured person who is more likely to call the police and commence a mobilization of the law.

The fourth independent variable is social control. Black did advocate that the law was indeed a component of social control, but equally, so too, are such factors as " etiquette, custom, ethics, and bureaucracy…[thus defining social control as] the normative aspect of social life that defines right and wrong" (Avakame, 1999, p.771). People are expected to be raised with certain values that are attained in school, church and within the family. These values thus provide us with a guide toward social control. The realization of right from wrong will dictate the physical path that one seeks in violating the law. Black pronounces that social control is perceived to be greater in private settings as opposed to public settings, whereas crimes are more likely to occur in the public realm than among intimates in private. Equally vital is the aspect of night versus day. Black proposes that a lack of social control, or criminal violations, are more apt to be committed during the cover of darkness than during the daylight hours. Therefore, Black concludes that the police are more likely to respond to requests for police service during the nighttime in the public realm.

From the definitions of the independent variables listed above, Black theorized that a wealthier person was more apt to call the police than a poorer person when witness to a crime and to see through that the offender was arrested, that a more educated person as compared to a lesser educated person when witness to a crime was more likely to call the police and to see that the offender was arrested and that a white person rather than a member of a minority group when witness to a crime was more likely to call the police and see the offender arrested. (Avakame, 1999). Black's theoretical predictions were far more extensive than what is presented here, but these are some of the more prominent propositions.

Edem F. Avakame and James J. Faye, professors of criminal justice at Temple University along with Candace McCoy, professor of criminal justice at Rutgers University utilized empirical data and calculation in an attempt to determine the validity of Black's proposed theories. Utilizing data from the 1992-1994 National Crime Victimization Survey they selected 48,114 respondents that were victims to crimes of rape, attempted rape, other sexual assault, and aggravated assault. The victims' relationship with the attacker allegedly was at the level of an acquaintance or otherwise knew their attacker. Victims of these particular crimes did indeed exist where the attacker was a stranger. However, in these cases arrests grossly lacked and the necessary data to prove Black's morphology theory was also lacking.

Interestingly, the results showed additional factors that determined police services and eventual arrests that Black did not consider, such as the victim's willingness to cooperate with police, the offender's demeanor and if the offender was present when police arrived. But, the victim's willingness to cooperate does indeed parallel Black's theory with respect to all the independent variables mentioned. One's willingness to cooperate will undoubtedly correlate to one's social stratification, morphology, culture and non-legal social control. Therefore, Black concluded that a victim who is categorized as wealthier, more educated, of higher social strata is more likely to cooperate with police and demand arrest. If cooperation is lacking, as being displayed by the victim from a police perspective, is it due to a lack of education, a lower social status with a decreased degree of social control? Is the level of cooperation determined from the police perspective or from the victim's perspective? This was a crucial factor that apparently was not considered by either Black nor Avakame, Fyfe nor McCoy.

What Avakame, Fyfe and McCoy did determine based upon their findings was that stratification as an independent variable was mixed. Minorities of such crimes as listed above were more likely to call the police than whites, however, arrests rates for white victims was higher than for those minority victims. With respect to morphology, the lack of stranger on

50

stranger crime was not compiled due to the lack of arrest data available. But, what the data did reveal is that the greater the relational distance between the victim and the offender the more likely the police would be notified and the more likely that arrest would be completed. Black's independent variable of culture exhibited that the people of less culture, and or less education were actually more likely to call the police for service, but it was the person of greater cultural values as perceived by the police that received the fullest quantity of the law in that arrest rates for these victims were higher. And finally, Black's independent variable of social control saw higher rates of calls for police service amongst victimization that took place within private quarters and they were more likely to result in arrest. Victimizations during the night time hours did increase as Black theorized and were more likely to call the police, however, arrest rates were lower than that of those victimized during the day in private settings.

Black's theorizations, now over three decades ago, do indeed support the hypothesis that America's police was founded within the realm of the political power elite. Those who controlled politics and the economy, from a historical perspective, sought nothing more than to protect their own elitist interests through political influence and power, so as to keep the threat of social disorder in control amongst the lower classes, to which such a coercive foundation has formulated the strategies of policing within the United States as we know it today. The findings of Avakame, Fyfe and McCoy undoubtedly provide mixed reflections upon Black's theories. Unquestionably though, Black neglected such immeasurable factors as individual police perspectives upon victims and offenders, which in fact incorporates the strategies of policing as we know it today as put forth within the hypothesis. It is evident to determine that the findings support that the police oblige the white victim far greater than the minority victim as indicated by corresponding arrest rates. This indeed speaks for itself that the white majority, the power elite

51

receives a greater quantity of law, as advocated by Black over thirty years ago, as compared to the socially insignificant.

Chapter IV

The Police and Crime Control: Pawns in a Political Game

Every symbol stands for something other than itself, and it also evokes an attitude, a set of impressions, or a pattern of events associated through time, through space, through logic, or through imagination with the symbol.

> Murray Edelman, 1964
> *Professor of Political Science*
> *University of Illinois*

Political Rhetoric and its Very Real Affect Upon Policing

Representation of the people for the people has lost its way within the progression of government in the United States. Many Americans believe that no such representation exists any longer amongst the American political arena, rather the politician is a narcissistic individual who pursues nothing more than self-interests to build upon an elitist empire, oftentimes in concert with other like politicians. The methodology utilized by the American politician is rhetoric, a powerful tool that employs symbolism as the impetus behind social change. More simply put, "this means that subjects and symbols may be deployed strategically...with little concern for an accompanying policy agenda" (Walker & Waterman, 2008, p.344). Rhetorical symbolism can incite the people toward change, too often demanding change for a problem that does not really exist or exacerbating an event to a disproportionate level; crime control is one such issue. Crime is used by political platforms to create and increase public support. For example, President Clinton's proclamation that he would place 100,000 new police officers on the streets of America to fight crime or President George W. Bush announcing shortly after the September 11, 2001, attacks the immediate need to suspend Fourth Amendment rights in order to effectively combat terrorism. "In this way, crime becomes a symbolic issue for these political actors...symbols drive their meaning not from content, but from the value people attach to them...in other words...politicians...use symbols to convey a value, an attitude, or a sentiment without having to provide details or substantive policies" (Oliver & Marion, 2008, p.4). Social change is often the result of political symbolism with no ethical guiding force nor resultant policy. Rhetorical symbolism charged with political self-interests has consumed American policing that has resulted in unfulfilled agendas as well as the deployment of definitive strategies that continuously affects policing throughout the United States all in the name of votes. The police are pawns in a political game.

Steven Lab puts forth that "there is no set crime prevention policy in the United States, except to investigate the crime, arrest and prosecute the offender, and punish the individual for his or her transgressions" (2004, p.681). This is indeed a bold statement that would upset many academicians, police executives and politicians who, collectively, over the years created, implemented and or supported such recognized crime prevention initiatives as Drug Awareness Resistance Education (D.A.R.E), community oriented policing and the adaptation of a three strikes law with respect to offender recidivism to name a few. Can these programs be actually categorized as a national effort within the realm of crime prevention, or rather ideas that were inflamed by politicians across the nation, both at the national and local levels, and sustained in the face of declining support and failure encapsulated in political rhetoric aimed at the ignorant voter?

Let us first examine in greater depth the well known initiative that is too often believed to be and recognized as a *national* crime prevention policy, D.A.R.E. There is no federal policy that governs the D.A.R.E program, albeit there is an entity referred to as D.A.R.E. America, a private national organization that oversees the entire D.A.R.E program and its political determination to sustain such a program, however, this is not a federal program governed by federal policy. The program is largely funded by private donations.

The D.A.R.E. program commenced in Los Angeles during the tenure of police chief Daryl F. Gates. Having been sued by the American Civil Liberties Union for utilizing undercover police officers in high schools across the city to combat an ever-increasing drug abuse problem, Chief Gates oversaw the creation of D.A.R.E. in 1983, as an alternative to combat continued drug

55

abuse among children within the City of Los Angeles (Gates, 1992). This so-called opposite approach, that being crime prevention through education rather than detect, arrest and prosecute, was accepted by the school board, but ironically it was the political realm that was not that enthusiastic about the program. In the early 1980s, the drug problem and the utilization of education to warn about the negative aspect of drugs was not on the forefront of a politician's agenda to win over constituents. The American public was well aware of the drug abuse problem and arrest and prosecute was still the call of the day. However, Gates finally won over the Los Angeles city council for funding for D.A.R.E. with his individual success stories from varied inner-city children. He brought the program to a national awareness by meeting with President Reagan and President Bush. First Lady Nancy Reagan's famed slogan, "Just Say No," began the politicization of a national anti-drug abuse campaign that eventually led to the explosion of the D.A.R.E. program across the nation (1992). A national office, outside of federal government control, was eventually established. Federal funding was made available through the 1986 Drug-Free Schools and Communities Act of which much of this particular funding was set aside for D.A.R.E. programs among various municipalities (Ennet, Flewelling, Ringwalt, & Tobler, 1994), however, the program itself has never been incorporated as a federally mandated crime prevention policy.

It is unknown if Daryl Gates' desire was to nationally politicize his drug resistance education program, but that is what precisely occurred. In 1988, then Republican nominee Vice President George Bush met with Gates during his election for president and accepted all Gates had to convey regarding the very real drug abuse problem the nation's youth were facing at the time (Gates, 1992); D.A.R.E. was now a political entity being captured by every politician. The popularity of D.A.R.E. ignited political rhetoric winning over the general public by proclaiming

56

that drug resistance education was the method best used to save our youth from the drug dealer that was on every street corner throughout the United States. The author is not suggesting that the drug problem across the United States was being exaggerated by politics at the commencement of the D.A.R.E. explosion. The author recognizes and accepts the very real drug abuse concerns at that time and the very prevalent concerns that continue into the twenty-first century. It is however, a travesty that the politicization of D.A.R.E. continues over twenty years after its inception regardless of literature that clearly suggests the program's failures and inadequacies. As concluded in the famed literary meta-analysis by Ennet, Flewelling, Ringwalt and Tobler, as early as 1994, "the results of this meta-analysis suggest that D.A.R.E.'s core curriculum effect on drug use relative to whatever drug education (if any) was offered...is not statistically significant" (1994, p.1398). Additionally, the study concluded perhaps the most damaging evidence to support the notion that D.A.R.E had become entrenched in political symbolism, "DARE's limited influence on adolescent drug use behavior contrasts with the program's popularity and prevalence" (1994, p.1399). Why then do politicians continue to support a program that in the face of empirically compiled data suggests its ineffectiveness and in some cases a negative overall effect? "The only reason to do so is because it is politically palatable to back a failed program that has a strong national organization behind it that has convinced the public that the program works" (Lab, 2004, p.687).

The fever of community oriented policing took off with the rhetoric of President William Clinton in 1994 who, in an effort to take political control of crime, a topic usually reserved for a Republican platform, promised to put 100,000 additional police officers on the streets of America through a new program incorporated into the government's Department of Justice. Community policing was the new paradigm for the politician who could capitalize on an

57

approach that was going to integrate communities that would ward off racial tensions between minority groups and the police, creating the perception that the police are equal stakeholders in the overall betterment of a respective community alongside its citizens and organizations. This was beautifully constructed political rhetoric that captivated the public into thinking that unique partnerships with the police would be formed and crime would finally be controlled. In 1994, such rhetoric resulted in the creation of the Office of Community Oriented Policing(COPS) under the Clinton administration. Monies were available for law enforcement agencies of all size to seek grants in order to hire additional police officers. The face of policing across the United States appeared to be changing in a variety of ways (community policing will be discussed further in subsection 3 of Chapter IV). The politically charged offices of police chiefs across America were quick to jump aboard the new political paradigm where many possessed no knowledge nor did they receive any guidance from the Office of Community Oriented Policing. This result was pure rhetorical symbolism at its finest and it effected change within the methodology of policing all across the United States using taxpayer dollars. There were no "clear guidelines for the use of these funds [COPS grants] or a clear philosophy regarding the expectations of these officers" (Lab, 2004, p.688). But, none of that really was a concern. The politician, both local and nationally, compounded upon the fact that COPS was placing more and more newly hired police officers on the streets and that made the public feel safe, which made the public feel positive about the politician who made that possible. "It was easier to point to the number of officers as a sign of success, rather than to the impact of the officers on crime and community disorder" (2004, p.688). The political rhetoric need not have called for any further evaluation, for police officers were being hired through the administration of federal monies and that was the only result necessary to support the constituents.

In 1994 California politicians who supported legislation for a three strikes law were victorious when the state's voters adopted the law in the November election (Datta & Kelly, 2009). The law established the foundation for nearly every state in the union, including the federal government, to soon follow after Californians proclaimed a political victory in their fight against crime. The law is outlined as follows:

Offenders who commit one violent or serious felony offense are subject to harsher sentences for any subsequent crime. In the case of a second violent or serious offense, the offender would receive a sentence length double what the typically suggested sentence would be. Additionally, property crimes, specifically theft, become felony offenses in the event that an individual has a prior conviction of the same nature. For example, suppose an individual is convicted of two counts of auto theft once and is then arrested for grand theft a decade after his release from prison. The charge, which can be considered a misdemeanor and which carries a one year sentence, is elevated to felony status and the offender would be sentenced to 2 years imprisonment. Additionally, the offender must serve a minimum of 80% of the sentence before having the chance of parole. Any offender who is arrested and charged with a violent or serious felony offense that has two or more of the same convictions can be and typically is sentenced to a minimum of 25 years and a maximum of life in prison in California's judicial system (2009).

Politicians capitalized upon crime and the fear of becoming a victim for the law-abiding citizen by denouncing the broken criminal justice system and its leniency for repeat offenders. At the time there was little data to support that such a law would in fact deter criminal activity, but again that was not the concern. The political rhetoric of the day was paramount, such legislation was imperative in order to persuade the public that the law would deter criminal activity, thus providing the politician with the necessary continued support under the guise of crime fighter. More importantly, the political advocate of such legislation did not consider the overwhelming financial factor that would be involved in such a symbolic gesture in the fight against crime. Simple logic would have concluded that such a law may indeed increase the prison population to some degree; not all offenders will be deterred, assuming that the law will have some degree of success. There were no corresponding enactments to increase the building of prisons nor increase the budgets of the prisons. The three strikes legislation actually resulted in a greater strain on prisons throughout the nation with respect to overcrowding, personnel and maintenance (Datta & Kelly, 2009). Some in the law enforcement community began to argue that the law actually increased violence against law enforcement officers due to the repeat offender realizing that apprehension by police will result in a life in prison.

The three strikes law is yet another example of political rhetoric resulting in symbolism that paved the way for very real policy changes that negatively impacted the role of law enforcement in the United States . A study focusing on crime in California between 1984-2004 concluded "…that the three strikes legislation has no statistical significance in its deterrence suggests that on the whole, violent crime is generally harder to prevent than other types of crime" (Datta & Kelly, 2009, p.35). "Politicians, however, are not shy about pointing to this legislation as a sign that they are tough on crime" (Lab, 2004, p.687).

Simply put, rhetorical symbolism that results in policy change does not concern itself with longevity nor success, only what appears to be successful such as noted above. Additionally, there are and were those crime fighting programs that were quick responses to an immediacy that the politician perceived as desired by the public, but the realization of failure was quick and a quiet abandonment usually prevailed. For example, President George Bush's design and implementation of the Department of Homeland Security resulting in the integration of eight major federal agencies. These agencies included: U.S. Border Patrol, Federal Emergency Management Agency, Transportation Security Administration, Citizenship and Immigration Services, United States Coast Guard, Immigration and Customs Enforcement, United States Secret Service and the Office of Inspector General (United States, 2009). Shortly after the terrorist attacks of September 11, 2001, the president moved quickly to give the American people the sense that the government was going to create radical change to protect our nation. Little evaluation went into the design of the oversized "super agency" (Lab, 2004, 688), but that was not the concern of politicians who rallied together in united bipartisanship so as to exhibit to the American people that the government was going to take a harsh enforcement effort against those who wish to enter our nation and do us harm. Within two years after implementation the Bush administration was seeking to cut the budget of the Department of Homeland Security by $500 million before it was even at its intended level. Today, the department appears to be part of the American federal system, but its emphasis has decreased due to the Iraq war and the fight against terrorism in Afghanistan (Lab, 2004). Again, the political rhetoric of the day shall prevail.

Steven Lab presents four premises that politicians prefer when formulating rhetorical strategy with regard to crime control and policing. Generally, politics is shortsighted with little to no forethought. Rhetoric captures the moment, usually sensationalized by the media. What is paramount this week will be forgotten next week. If it is a topic that endures, such as crime control, symbolism results with empty promises, abandoned initiatives and continued strategies in the face of failure. Therefore, the politician generally will capture rhetoric that fits easily into the following: 1. *Politicians look for immediate results that will help them be reelected,* such as putting more police on the street in the COPS program, rather than a long term evaluation to see if the increase in police actually decreased crime, 2. *The emphasis for politicians is on what can be easily counted,* such as the three strikes law and the number of offenders being placed back in prison, 3. *Politicians emphasize those policies and actions that play well in 15 second sound bites,* such as we are going to get tough on crime, 4. *Political decisions are always focused on the issue of the moment,* such as George Bush's reaction to decrease Fourth Amendment protections in order to better protect the American people from terrorists along with the creation of the super agency, Department of Homeland Security after the September 11, 2001 attacks against the United States (2004, p.685).

The interests of the state have indeed become the self-interests of the politician, yet in a collective manner amongst all politicians. As described above, "political decisions have been made which serve the interests of politicians and policy makers. The decisions either ignore established knowledge or make unfounded assumptions to achieve what is perceived to be the most politically expedient course of action. What is lacking is any attempt to truly prevent crime and other societal problems" (Lab, 2004, p.689).

Presidential Influence

The democratic values as established within the United States theoretically leaves the states and the municipalities to police themselves, clearly this literary review has established that this is indeed not so. In his 1929, state of the union address, President Herbert Hoover remarked, "It may be said that the larger responsibility for the enforcement of laws against crime rests with state and local authorities and it does not concern the federal government. But, it does concern the President of the United States, both as a citizen and as the one whom rests the primary responsibility of leadership for the establishment of standards of law enforcement in this country" (Oliver, 2002, p.3). President Hoover established a precedent that would be utilized by many future presidents that were yet to be born; crime control and the police can be controlled by the highest office in the land through mere words. In 1947, President Truman remarked of crime and the Constitution in his state of the union address and 14 years later President Kennedy incorporated crime into his state of the union address, resulting in every sitting president after

Kennedy to do so as well (2002). Partisanship consumes the presidency, the sitting president is indeed representative of the party platform that he aligns himself with, therefore, "...control of the executive branch infers partisan control of the coercive force of the democratic state" (Walker & Waterman, 2008, p.346). As discussed earlier in Chapter I, a true democratic state cannot exist without a coercive arm of the government protecting established freedoms. Presidential influence establishes the direction for that coercive arm, more commonly known as the police, amongst the people. The power of the president's words and his party became a steadfast "...American institution within a decade after the establishment of the U.S. government" (Oliver & Marion, 2008, p.2).

The public's perception of crime and its level of importance is directly affected by the level of importance and placement of crime control as put forth by the sitting president's agenda and the rhetorical symbolic policy announced. This agenda, or lack of, has a direct impact upon local and state law enforcement nationally. For example, in 1929, when President Hoover was the first president to speak about crime issues facing the nation at that time, "he detailed the problems of overcrowded federal prisons, prohibition, the problem with law enforcement and observance, organized crime, and corruption..." (Oliver, 2002, p.8). Hoover's address resulted in the creation of the National Commission on Law Observance and Enforcement, or more historically known as the Wickersham Commission, which was given the task of investigating the causes of criminal activity and alcohol related influences across the United States. One such result of the commission's report was the recommendation of extensive reforms within policing with respect to training, selection and education in addition to the recognition of the existence of widespread brutality as a deployed and accepted tactic among the policing field (Miller, 2000). Presidential influence upon policing had become another democratic value incognito.

63

A president is considered as the most influential political figure at any given time. There is simply no other politician or rhetoric that will be followed to the degree that the president is. The president has the ability to set and control agendas with the issue of crime control and how the police respond to such statements. "One of the key reasons for the president's preeminent position in agenda setting is because of his command of public attention, which can be converted into pressure on other government officials to adopt the president's agenda" (Oliver, 2002, p.5).

An empowering example is that of President Harry S. Truman, who was warned by his political advisers not to speak on race relations and the apparent tensions and segregation that was still prevalent throughout the nation still looming from the Civil War. However, in 1947, against such advice, Truman made the following statement in his state of the union address, "We have recently witnessed in this country numerous attacks upon the constitutional rights of individual citizens as a result of racial and religious bigotry...the will to fight these crimes should be in the hearts of every one of us" (Oliver, 2002, p.8). Truman's statement moved forward to establish the President's Committee on Civil Rights, thus bringing to the realm of the presidency the topic of race relations and its comingling with crime, providing for a focus on law enforcement practices throughout the nation (The American, 1952).

President Kennedy's state of the union address in 1961 brought attention to race relations once again in addition to organized crime and a heightened awareness of juvenile crime. Kennedy brought about the norm of speaking on the issue of crime control with every president thereafter remarking on crime control issues to some degree. Every president varied on the level of importance with regard to crime, depending upon the party's platform and the president's political agenda. As of 2002 President Clinton remarked the most about crime with a total of 62 sentences being devoted to the topic of crime in his 1994 state of the union address. Although

Clinton is credited with establishing the Office of Community Oriented Policing and vowing to place an additional 100,000 police officers on the streets of America, Clinton's agenda for reducing crime was very symbolic (Oliver & Marion, 2008). "He [Clinton] often spoke about crime issues in a general nature rather than proposing specific policies and ideas for deterring criminal activity" (2008, p.6). As noted earlier, Clinton's Office of Community Oriented Policing and his COPS grants provided no "clear guidelines for the use of these funds or a clear philosophy regarding the expectations of these officers" (Lab, 2004, p.688). This was the result of presidential symbolism at its finest all in an effort to maintain public support.

Clinton was by no means the exception, other than his spoken word being perhaps far more eloquent as compared to previous presidents. Sitting presidents, as well as those seeking the office during the electoral process, would often use "..executive orders to portray their concerns about increasing crime rates, rather than propose tangible policies...and use symbolic rhetoric about crime to help get them elected"(Oliver & Marion, 2008, p.6). A president is the party and the platform to be conveyed is of the utmost importance for reelection and or maintaining the particular party in the office. Symbolic rhetoric is used to gain confidence in the public that the crime issue will be tackled. "In doing so, the parties propose few actual specific proposals for change but rely instead on general statements that indicate broad concerns" (2008, p.7) regardless of the actual, empty, resultant effect that such general statements may have upon law enforcement procedures and strategies. The values of President Truman got lost over time somewhere within the oval office, "If something is wrong, the thing to do is to dig it out, find why it is wrong, and take sensible steps to put it right"(The American, 1952). This is not a concern of the presidency, simply remarking on crime control can satisfy the agenda's objective, that of keeping the public fooled in believing that the police are protecting and serving the public in their best interests so that the current party can continue to remain in control.

Community Policing: A Political Fad

Community policing has become the all too familiar slogan of contemporary law enforcement throughout the nation. Ask a police executive of any agency within the United States if his/her agency employs community policing practices and the answer will most certainly be yes. This does not necessarily mean that community policing within its true sense and practice is actually being deployed. As a matter of fact there are numerous police executives that do not have the necessary theoretical and organizational knowledge that is necessary to implement such a program. Why then would a police executive overseeing an agency firmly stand by his/her affirmative answer that community policing is indeed being practiced within the agency? Simply put, political influence. The new paradigm that was born in the early 1990s was not of police innovation, but rather was the result of political symbolism. Undoubtedly, the police were not succeeding at the job of crime control toward the end of the twentieth century and a new approach toward policing practices was desperately needed on the very near horizon. The Professional Era of policing was still clinging to life, more so in the larger urban agencies. There was a need for a paradigm shift within policing once again, but policing in general is far less adaptive to its surrounding, ever-evolving environment. The politician, however, is keenly aware of the continuous evolution of society and the people served. The politician's adaptiveness has evolved into an art and to some degree has emerged as a science. The politician took advantage of the moment, captured the fears of the people, seized it and the new era of community oriented policing was born out of the fervor of the politics of the day.

Under President Clinton, the community policing concept emerged out of the 1994 Violent Crime Control and Law Enforcement Act (Morabito, 2008). The act paved the way for the Office of Community Oriented Policing (COP) to be created under the auspice of the Department of Justice. The office was responsible for the distribution of community oriented policing grants to thousands of agencies in an effort to support President Clinton's 1992 pledge to place 100,000 additional police officers on the streets. More than eight billion dollars was distributed to "...more than 90 percent of American police agencies serving populations larger than 25,000 [that] reported adopting community policing activities and strategies" (2008, p.469). Being that community policing was such a new and ambiguous concept, the Office of Community Oriented Policing defined COP as

A philosophy that promotes organizational strategies, which support the systematic use of partnerships and problem-solving techniques, to proactively address the immediate conditions that give rise to public safety issues such as crime, social disorder, and fear of crime (2009).

This definition would essentially require police agencies to change not only organizationally but to adapt to a new way of policing involving procedural changes, newly formed divisions and officers solely dedicated to the practice of community policing, which would collectively impact the daily operations of a department. In theory, if a police executive was to refer to his/her agency as one that was effectively and efficiently deploying and practicing community oriented policing, the department would have had to undergone extensive restructuring. Most did not.

A 2003 study compiled by Professor Max Bromley, of the University of South Florida, supports the fact that most agencies, which claimed to practice COP, were far less involved than the full philosophical definition actually called for. The study examined a total of 1,452 city law enforcement agencies. The study revealed that out of 288 agencies with a size of 50-99 sworn personnel, 37.5% had a written COP policy, whereas 54.4 % did not. Surprisingly, 87.2% out of the 288 agencies did claim to have full-time officers devoted solely to COP. Yet, only 33.3% of the agencies conducted at least eight hours of in-service training on community oriented policing principles. It was far easier to incorporate training at the recruit level with 68.8% of the departments doing so. Only 43.1% of the agencies claimed to have formed partnerships with community organizations as called for in the definition. And, only 50.3% of agencies actually employed problem-solving techniques as again outlined within the definition (2003).

This data clearly suggests that police departments are not fully implementing the philosophy of COP. Why? Clinton's Office of Community Oriented Policing and his COPS grants provided no "clear guidelines for the use of these funds or a clear philosophy regarding the expectations of these officers" (Lab, 2004, p.688). This was the result of presidential symbolism at its finest all in an effort to maintain politically motivated public support. Most police executives are ill-informed and ill-skilled to implement such a widespread, structural and operational change within their departments. However, the police chief who can say that COP is working within their department has captured the essence of COP, the politics of the day. Professor Melissa Schaefer Morabito, of the University of Massachusetts, summed up the entire essence of the COP program quite well in the following statement;

"Police administration itself has been described as a political process because it requires balancing leadership, accountability and political responsiveness. In the majority of localities in the USA, the tenure of the police chief is tied to the approval of the mayor or the city manager. To maintain job security, chiefs may choose to implement policies and strategies such as community policing that promote the agendas of other local officials. In this political environment, the decision to implement community policing may be based on the wishes of actors such as the mayor or city manager rather than solely on an internal police decision-making process. Despite the relative importance of the political environment to the process of the adoption of community policing including applying for federal grants and the subsequent hiring and training of officers, this influence has been largely omitted from much of the community policing literature" (2008, p.469).

The fact is that numerous police chiefs and politicians throughout the country captured Clinton's symbolism and took it to the fullest extent possible. The art of instituting varied yet empty programs and assigning officers to numerous unsuccessful and fruitless tasks as well as providing lip service to politicians, all of which "have been lumped together under the name community policing unilaterally by the police"(Sklansky, 2006, p.90), was the job of the police executive with no real measurement. Success with regard to a rhetorically symbolic program is of no concern to the police executive. Keeping the elected officials supplied with much rhetoric for party platforms in the arena of crime control, in turn, keeps the police executive employed.

Mayors and city managers across America continue to push for COP due to its appealing philosophies to the communities served that the police are working side by side with community leaders and organizations, working together to reduce crime. Additionally, elected officials certainly welcome any form of federal financial assistance and will claim what is necessary to seize it including the police chiefs who work for them (Morabito, 2008). The politician, in his/her 15 second sound bite, will proclaim that more police officers are on the street under COP funding, but has little to no concern nor inquiry as to whether the program has had any impact whatsoever on the reduction of crime (Lab, 2004). According to the Office of Community Oriented Policing at the end of Fiscal year 2008, approximately 117, 000 additional police officers were on patrol due to federal COP grants.

Policing in America has witnessed numerous paradigm shifts, none of which has been sustained. Undoubtedly, with the ominous threat of terrorism in the twenty-first century, community policing will too dissipate. A new paradigm for American policing is on the horizon; fads of all kinds eventually are replaced. The politician will capture a moment with an exciting party platform and it shall once again invade law enforcement and police executives all across

69

the nation will succumb to the politics of the day. Aside from any program research, evaluation or documented successes or failures or lack thereof, President Clinton's Office of Community Oriented Policing eventually provided for 117, 000 new police officers, but brought to the polls millions of votes. Now that is all that really mattered.

Bratton's Success Story: When Competent Police Leadership and Expertise Come Together Autonomy can Prevail

William J. Bratton, appointed police commissioner of the New York City Police Department in 1994, brought with him, to one of the most coveted yet controversial posts in all of law enforcement, unique and unparalleled ideologies unlike any other that America's most populated city had ever witnessed within the realm of crime fighting. Bratton began his career as a patrol officer in Boston and with unusual speed rose through the ranks to become the police chief/commissioner of the Massachusetts Bay Transit Authority Police, Boston Police Department, Metropolitan District Commission Police Department of Massachusetts, New York City Transit Police Department, New York City Police Department and finally the Los Angeles Police Department (Bratton, 1998). His no nonsense approach to crime reduction made it look almost simple. Casting doubt upon many major theories about the role of police in society and the causation of major crime, it made many in the field of policing wonder why this approach was not acted upon sooner. Bratton did not succumb to the politics of the day nor did he partake in the political symbolism that engrossed law enforcement in the latter half of the twentieth century. Indeed, he was keenly aware of politics and learned how to balance it. However, Bratton had ideas and solidified plans for New York City, and he moved forward putting those plans into action that resulted in a drastic reduction in crime for the Big Apple. He put politics in its place, outside the realm of crime fighting, which made him one of the most successful and respected law enforcement executives of the twentieth century.

Bratton's New York success story began under the streets of New York City when he was appointed as the police chief of the New York City Transit Authority Police Department in 1990 (Bratton, 1998). Bratton took command of a 4,000 member law enforcement agency that was charged with all policing services in a subway system that was plagued with panhandlers, homelessness, fare beaters, youth disorder, urination and defecation, robberies of patrons, robberies of transit authority personnel, drug and alcohol abusers and the mentally ill (Bratton & Kelling, 1998). The past regime of the transit authority police considered many of these disorder issues minor quality of life concerns and social concerns where the police had no business getting involved. Guided by political rhetorical symbolism that consumed law enforcement in the latter half of the twentieth century, police executives only saw the big picture, the same picture that the politician saw. Large scale rhetoric was the only political platform to pursue with respect to law enforcement, for it captured the public's interest and secured votes, such as the approaching community policing paradigm. Taking small steps and proclaiming to attend to the minor disorder and social issues so that larger crime concerns would cease to blossom was not a good fit for the 15 second political sound bite where symbolism would prevail, leaving law enforcement once again with no plan. The transit authority was desperate to solve its crime issues due to declining ridership but had no plan. Bratton and his team, to include George L. Kelling, brought with him to the subways of New York City a simplistic policing strategy, outside of politics, that not only worked for the city under a city, but would eventually work for the entire city.

71

The plan was simple, incorporate James Q. Wilson's broken windows theory that advocated attending to quality of life issues as well as small disorder issues. Over time larger crime concerns would soon dissipate (Bratton & Kelling, 1998). In conjunction with the broken windows theory they developed a three prong approach:

- Develop the idea into a plan of action

- Apply the plan in the New York City Subway system

- Apply new policies governing police leadership, management and organizational structure where accountability at all levels is monitored (1998).

Bratton's approach was contradictory to the politically controlled policing that had become commonplace among law enforcement executives. First, focusing on the small quality of life issues and social concerns was not paramount from a political perspective. Second, having an actual plan with parallel policy was unheard of. Third, providing command staff with defined tasks and agendas, rather than leaving police executives pondering as to what the guidelines actually were, if any existed at all, and providing for accountability from management at all levels.

Bratton's ideologies violated the basic tenets of "the reigning crime control policy view that had been developing throughout the 1950s and 1960s and made explicit by President Johnson's Crime Control Commission" (Bratton & Kelling, 1998, p.1219). Corresponding precisely with political agendas, this policy view saw the "police as law enforcement officers, the front end of the criminal justice system whose business is serious crime – arresting offenders...the police got out of the business of minor offenses" (1998, p.1219). Regardless, Bratton moved forward with his order maintenance policy through a zero tolerance approach. All minor violations of drunkenness, public urination, fare beaters, etc. would be dealt with by police. The police would utilize policing again, not just law enforcement, making the business of the police every quality of life issue within the transit system. Bratton's order maintenance "…was an especially significant part of reclaiming the subway and reducing crime" (1998, p.1220).

Bratton's achievements within the New York subway system were brought to light when he was appointed the commissioner of the New York City Police Department in 1994 (Bratton, 1998). Not leaving the transit police behind, Bratton's large-scale plan brought together the New York City Transit Police, New York City Housing Police and the New York City Police all into one agency, the largest municipal police agency in the nation (Bratton & Kelling, 1998). His order maintenance program that included "police tactics, organizational change, and administrative processes implemented in the transit police department foreshadowed changes in the New York City Police Department" (1998, p.1222).

Bratton's success in the transit system utilized the following methodologies:

- Transit police developed a specific set of interventions that included police tactics and changes in organizational structure and administrative processes

- The transit police called its own shots

- Continuous accountability paralleled intervention, which saw a steep reduction in crime (Bratton & Kelling, 1998).

Unlike political agendas laced with ill-defined symbolism, Bratton's methods were concise and tremendously effective with no ambiguity to stand in the way of success. He approached the city in the same manner. The New York City Police Department was a greater challenge however, infiltrated with the perception of corruption and still feeling the effects from the 1970s Knapp Commission investigations, the department had become consumed with protecting its reputation. Doing nothing was the order of business, doing nothing meant avoiding getting in

73

trouble; policing was an afterthought. Moving forward, Bratton proved that his methods, defying current and accepted politically motivated policing policy, could be overwhelmingly successful even on a large scale, such as New York City. Kelling remarked of Bratton's success in the following statement;

"Bratton approached his commissionership in New York City with a clear plan. He had an idea about how to prevent crime; he had an organizational strategy; he had an organizational strategy that he wanted to implement; and he pre-tested both with great success in New York City's subways. Again, as with the subway, he called his shots – both by demanding that mid-level managers be held accountable for crime reduction and by reducing plans for dealing with specific problems. One of the hallmarks in social science is that research should be guided by theory. Bratton's strategy was, in effect, management guided by theory. Innovations were implemented and crime dropped. A lot" (1998, p.1227).

Bratton's tenure as NYPD commissioner totaled only 27 months commencing in 1994. The NYPD crime statistics reveal comparisons between 1993 – 1997: (Henry, 2005).

Crime	1993	1997	%Change v. 1993
Murder	1,927	767	-60.2%
Rape	3,225	2,783	-13.7%
Robbery	85,892	44,335	-48.3%
Felony Assault	41,121	30,259	-26.4%
Burglary	100,936	54,866	-45.6%
Grand Larceny	85,737	55,686	-35.0%
Motor Vehicle Theft	111,662	51,312	-54.0%
Total	430,460	240,008	-44.24%

It is remarkable to have achieved such reductions in criminal activity in such a short time within a city of over eight million people. Within "20 months after Bratton took office, *New York Magazine* declared in a cover story, *The End of Crime As We Know It* (Bratton & Kelling, 1998, p.1218). Bratton's popularity boomed and this did not fit well with the political environment governed by Mayor Rudolph Giuliani. Rather than jumping on board with Bratton's success and exclaiming political victory in the war against crime in New York City, riding Bratton's coattails was not good enough for the mayor. Giuliani forced Bratton to resign within 27 months after taking office. It is mindboggling that Giuliani forced Bratton from office carrying with him a reputation as one the most successful police executives in the twentieth century. The conclusion is quite simple, all in the name of politics. Giuliani lost control of his police and that is simply not the American way. Bratton proved beyond a reasonable doubt that when competent police leadership and expertise come together, autonomy from political influence can prevail.

Conclusion

The Protect and To Serve Travesty

For most people, the police are government incarnate: the street-level embodiment of the state's monopolization of legitimate force.

> David Alan Sklansky, 2006
> Professor of Law
> University of California, Berkeley

Aristotle's philosophy outlining the rule of law and its necessity to effectively govern a civilized society has sustained in practice despite the collapse of the Roman Empire, unimaginable growth of the world's economic condition and the creation of a nation that claims to be the freest on the planet. Yet, a sustainable government cannot exist without social control and such control must be instituted through a coercive arm of the government. As noted as early as 1651, Thomas Hobbes proclaimed, "the growth of political economies spawned the concept for the need of "...an organized coercive power establishment... [to protect]...social freedoms...enforce contracts and property rights" (Daleiden, 2006, p.604). This proclamation by Hobbes provided a foundation for numerous future political philosophers and academicians to build upon and provide for a police concept such as English scholar Sir William Blackstone, 1765, who described specifically the police as, "the public police and economy" (2006, p.611), thus referring to an organized body of police to protect the community from not only murder and property crimes but equally as protector to the "...public infrastructure" (2006, p.611), and Scottish economist Adam Smith, 1763, who advocated for a form of policing as protector of the economy as well as Karl Marx, 1867, who spoke of the police as an institution of the state that was to be specifically utilized to maintain the existence of differing socioeconomic classes and of a police concept that involves professionalism, legality, reforms, and employs community relations (2006).

Reflecting upon the author's definition of the police as noted in Chapter I, the police are a non-excludable, non-divisible public good that are to protect and to serve social order in the interest of self-preservation for the existing body politic. This unorthodox definition embodies not only the political ideologies of the those as noted above but is still the prevailing truth today. Such control by the government was realized when Sir Robert Peel went before Parliament in

77

1829, arguing for his new concept of a paramilitary style state sponsored police force, supporting the notion that "those opposing the new police on the grounds of liberty gave credit to some parts of the population for the possession for the enjoyment of much more liberty than they actually possessed" (Dodsworth, 2006, p.446). To protect and to serve the will of the government had become a solid foundation for the necessity of a police structure.

The English policing concepts became well-established within America, but equally important was the fact that the people of the young nation stood steadfast with their new democratic ideology, which "prompted them to fear an institution imported from monarchial Europe" (Miller, 2000, p.31). It was this very fear that led to a desire by the American people to see that constables were to be appointed by local magistrates, local politicians or elected by the people. By demanding that early policing efforts be controlled through local politicians so as to avoid any similar concept of centralized state control, as compared to their English roots, Americans gave birth to a foundation of in-depth politically controlled, decentralized police forces all across the nation as well as at the soon to come federal level. Unknowingly, it would be this fear of monarchial control among the early settlers that resulted in the nemesis that plagues American law enforcement today, politics.

An examination of the hypothesis reveals that those who controlled politics and the economy, from a historical perspective, sought nothing more than to protect and serve their own elitist interests through political influence and power, thus formulating the strategies and deployment of policing within the United States as we know it today; this is precisely what the people asked for upon the birth of the nation's industrialized cities. Therefore, we need not wonder why the police are so entrenched and guided by the local and national politics of the day; the history of the police concept speaks for itself. But, to refer to the police, alone, as an American institution is not entirely correct. The police were born out of the necessity of a growing political economy that saw urbanization, immigration, racial tension and the development of social stratification as spawning disorder, thus creating an ever-present threat of collapse. The institution that was well-founded within the United States was indeed that policing is entrenched, guided and controlled by political symbolism. This is the protect and to serve travesty.

The following remarks by William Bratton, from his book entitled *Turnaround*, at the end of the twentieth century, offer hope that policing can stand alone and is not lost forever to the political institution that the United States has so overwhelmingly become.

"In terms of importance and potential and commitment, police in America are probably the most misunderstood entity in public life today. Old images exist, and, in truth, old-guard departments exist as well. But, as we approach the millennium, there is a new breed of police leader and a new breed of police officer. We need more of them.

I was privileged during my last half-dozen years in policing to work on the national and international stage, and I feel there is still more the police can do. The turnaround of the NYPD was the catalyst for the turnaround of New York City itself and offers a potential blueprint for the turnaround of the crime situation in the entire country. We clearly showed that when properly led, properly managed, and in effective partnership with the neighborhoods and the political leaders, police can effect great change. We have clearly shown that police can take back streets that were given up as lost for decades. The continuing challenge for American police leaders is to take them back in a lawful and respectful manner so that the behavior of the police reflects the civil behavior society expects of its citizens" (Bratton & Kelling, 1998, p.1231).

Los Angeles police officer Joseph S. Dorobeck's 1955 creation of the motto, *to protect and to serve*, remains hopeful.

References

Avakame, E. K., Fyfe, J. J., & McCoy, C. (1999). "Did you call the police? What did they do?"

    An empirical assessment of black's theory of mobilization of law. *Justice Quarterly, 16*(4),

    765-792.

Black, D.J. (1976). *The behavior of law.* New York, NY: Academic Press.

Bratton, W.J. (1998). *Turnaround.* (P. Knobler, Ed.). New York, NY: Random House, Inc.

Bratton, W.J., & Kelling, G.L. (1998). Declining crime rates: Insiders' views of the New York

    City story. *Journal of Criminal Law and Criminology, 88*(4), 1217-1231.

Bromley, M.L. (2003). Comparing campus and municipal police community policing practices.

    Journal of Security Administration, 26(2), 37-75.

Brown, M. C., & Warner, B. D. (1997). Immigrants, urban politics, and policing in 1900.

    American Sociological Review, 57(3), 293-305.

Constantine, S. (2008). The pirate, the governor and the secretary of state: Aliens, police and

    surveillance in early nineteenth-century Gibraltar. *English Historical Review, 123*(504),

    1166-1192.

Daleiden, J. R. (2006). A clumsy dance: The political economy of American police and policing.

    Policing: an International Journal of Police Strategies and Management, 29(4), 602-

    624.

Datta, A., & Kelly, J. (2009). Does three strikes really deter? A statistical analysis of its impact

    on crime rates in California. *College Teaching Methods and Styles Journal, 5*(1), 29-36.

Delisi, M. (2003). Conservatism and common sense: The criminological career of James Q.

    Wilson. *Justice Quarterly, 20*(3), 661-674.

DiCristina, B. (2000). Compassion can be cruel: Durkheim on sympathy and punishment. *Justice Quarterly, 17*(3), 485-494.

Dodsworth, F. (2007). Police and the prevention of crime: Commerce, temptation, and the body politic, from fielding to colquhoun. *The British Journal of Criminology, 47*(1), 439-454.

Edelman, M. (1964). *The symbolic use of politics*. Urbana, IL: University of Illinois Press.

Ennet, S. T., Flewelling, R. L., Ringwalt, C. L., & Tobler, N. S. (1994). How effective is drug abuse resistance education? A meta-analysis of project DARE outcome evaluations. *American Journal of Public Health, 84*(9), 1394-1401.

Gates, D. F. Shah. (1992). *Chief: My life in the lapd*. New York, NY: Bantam Books.

Goltz, J.W., Korosec, R., & Wolf, R. (2008). An analysis of factors affecting the implementation of small municipal police agencies: An open systems approach. *American Journal of Criminal Justice, 33*(2), 179-192.

Hasisi, B. (2008). Police, politics, and culture in a deeply divided society. *Journal of Criminal Law and Criminology, 98*(3), 1119-1145.

Harris, A.T. . (1999). Before the Bobbies: The night watch and police reform in metropolitan London, 1720-1830. *Canadian Journal of History, 34*(1), 110-112.

Henry, V. E. (2005). *Compstat management in the NYPD: Reducing crime and improving quality of life in New York City*. Paper presented at the 129th senior seminar visiting experts' papers, New York. Retrieved December 1, 2009, from The United Nations Asia and Far East Institute for the Prevention of Crime and the Treatment of Offenders Web site: www.unafei.or.jp/english/pdf/PDF_rms/no68/07/_Dr.%20Henry-1_p100-116.pdf

History of the FBI: Origins 1908-1910. (2009). Retrieved November 12, 2009, from Federal Bureau of Investigation Web site: http://www.fbi.gov

The origin of the lapd motto. (1963). Retrieved October 22, 2009, from Los Angeles Police

    Department Web site: http://www.lapdonline.org

Lab, S. P. (2004). Crime prevention, politics, and the art of going nowhere fast. *Justice*

    Quarterly, 21(4), 681-692.

Merton, R. K. (1997). On the evolving synthesis of differential association and anomie theory:

    A perspective from the sociology of science. *Criminology, 35*(3), 517-525.

Miller, W. (2000). The good, the bad & the ugly: Policing America. *History Today, (50)*8, 29-35.

Morabito, M. S. (2008). The adoption of police innovation: The role of the political environment.

    Policing: an International Journal of Police Strategies and Management, 31(3), 466-484.

Oliver, W. M., & Marion, N. E. (2008). Political party platforms: Symbolic politics and criminal

    justice policy. *Criminal Justice Policy Review, 19*(4), 397-413.

Parrish, T.L. (1994). Haymarket and hazard: The lonely politics of William Dean Howells.

    Journal of American Culture, 17(4), 23.

Sklansky, D.A. (2006). Private police and democracy. *The American Criminal Law Review,*

    43(1), 89-105.

Smith, P. (2008). Durkheim and criminology: Reconstructing the legacy. *The Australian and*

    New Zealand Journal of Criminology, 4(3), 333-344.

The American Presidency Project. (1952). *169-Commencement Address at Howard University by*

    President Harry S. Truman [research study]. Available from

    http://www.presidency.ucsb.edu/

The Office of Community Oriented Policing. (2009). *Department of Justice* [data file].

    Available from http://www.cops.usdoj.gov

United States Department of Homeland Security. (2009). *Homeland Security* [data file].

    Available from http://www.dhs.gov

Walker, L. D., & Waterman, R. W. (2008). Elections as focusing events: Explaining attitudes

    toward the police and the government comparative perspective. *Law and Society Review,*

    42(2), 337-365.

Wilson, J. Q. (1968). *Varieties in police behavior: The management of law and order in eight*

    communities. Cambridge, MA: Harvard University Press

Zedner, L. (2006). Policing before and after the police. *The British Journal of Criminology, 46,*

    78-96.

www.ingramcontent.com/pod-product-compliance
Lightning Source LLC
Chambersburg PA
CBHW060201290526
45789CB00003B/1104